American Spirit

Roe Ethridge

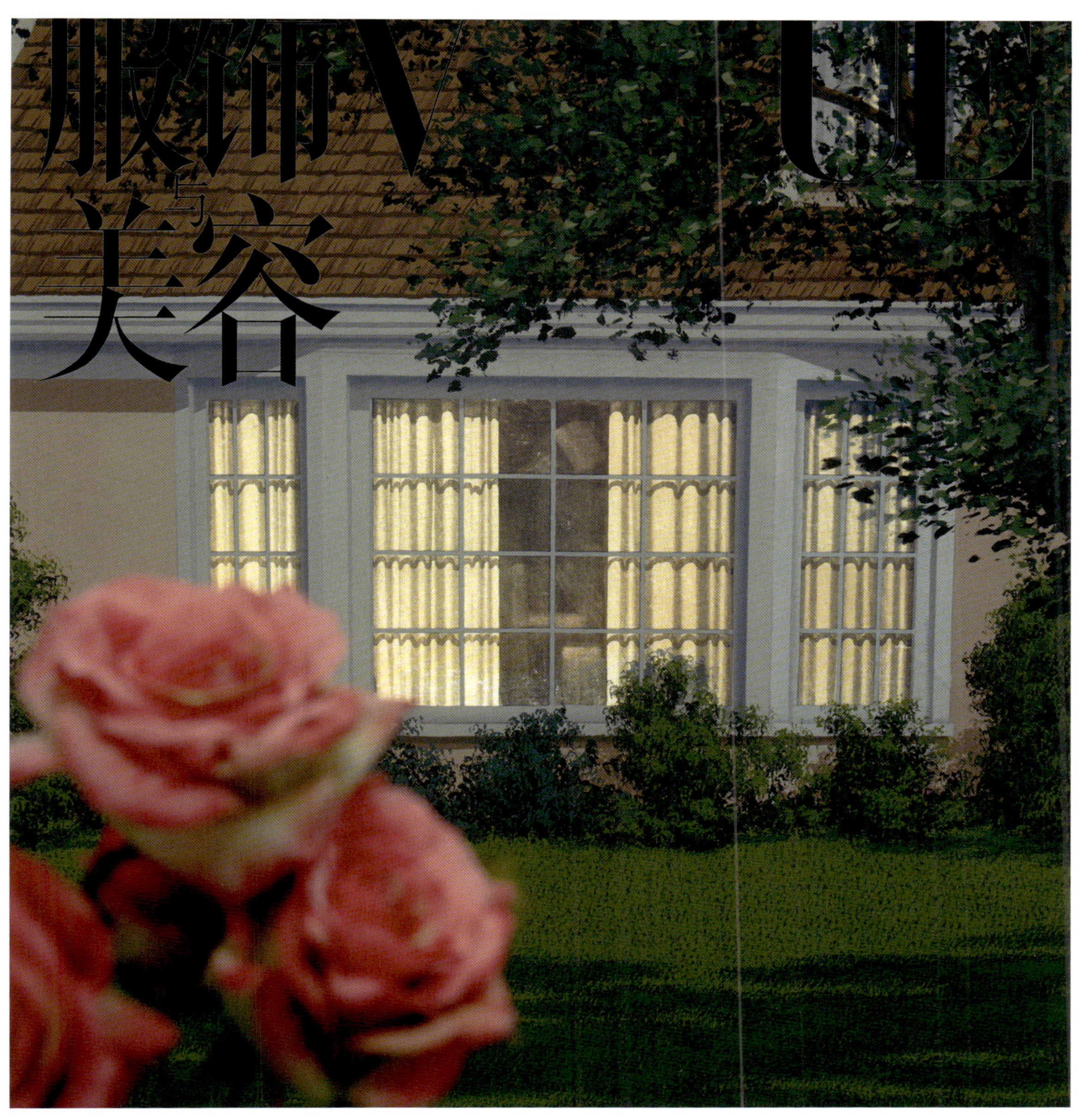
服饰与美容

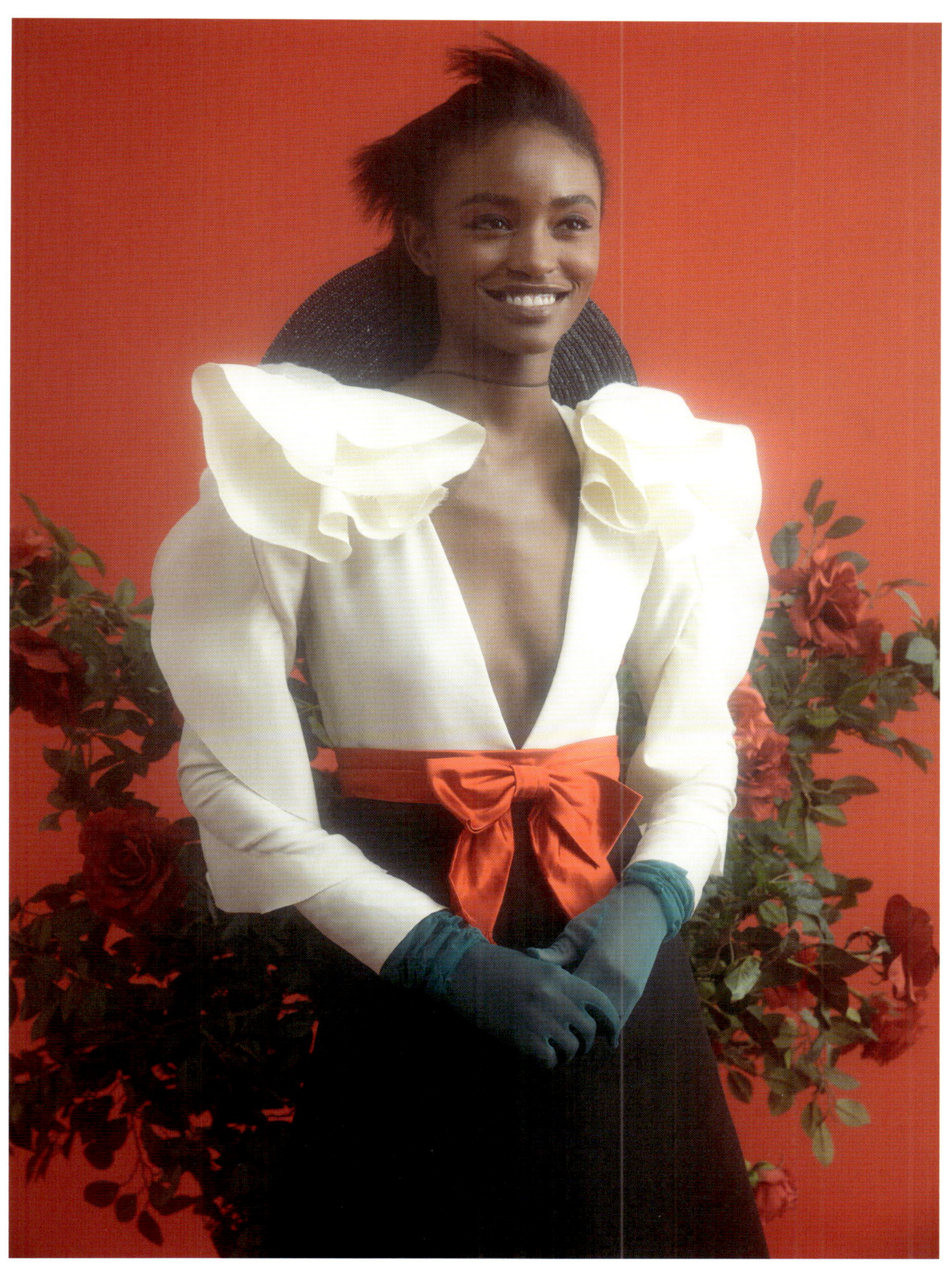

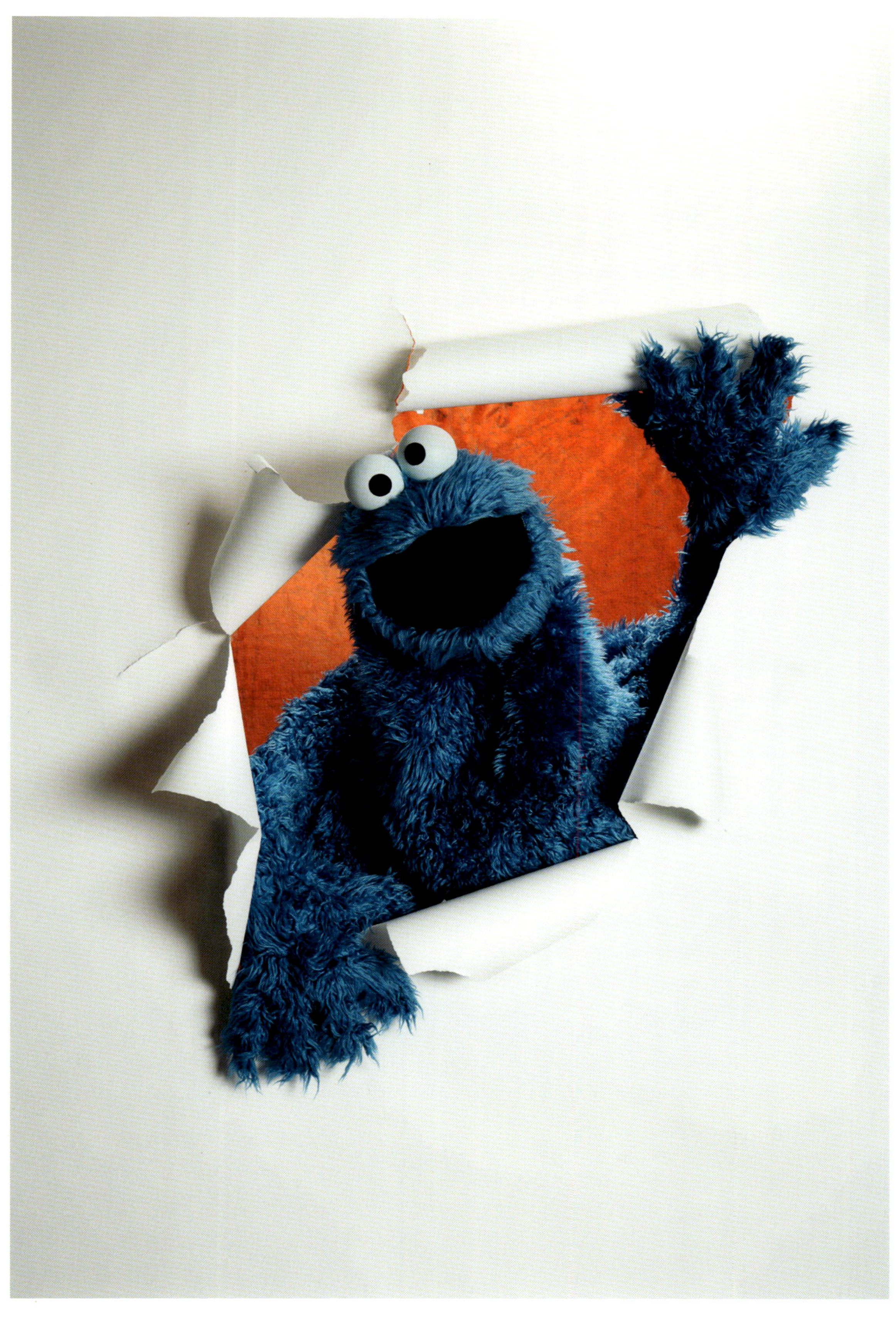

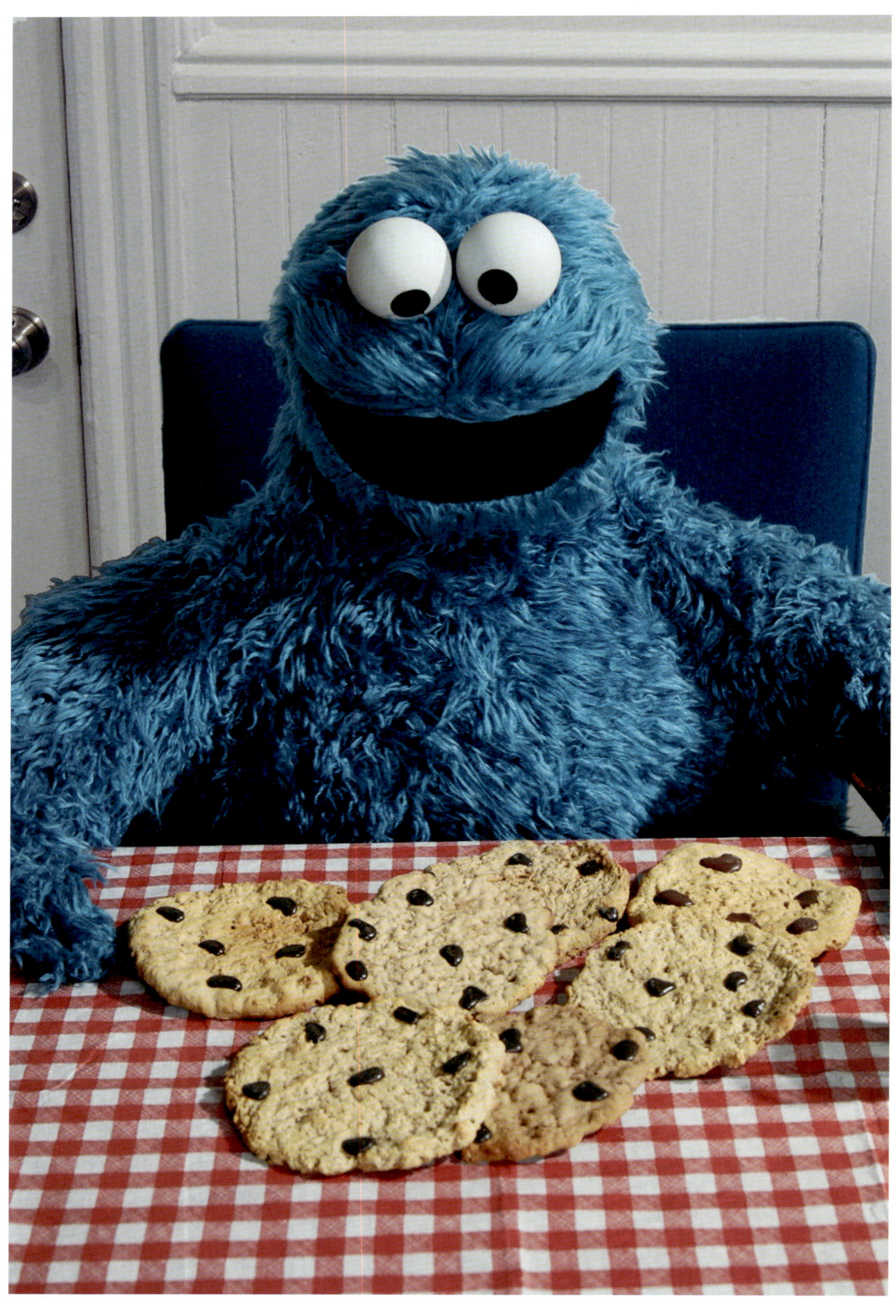

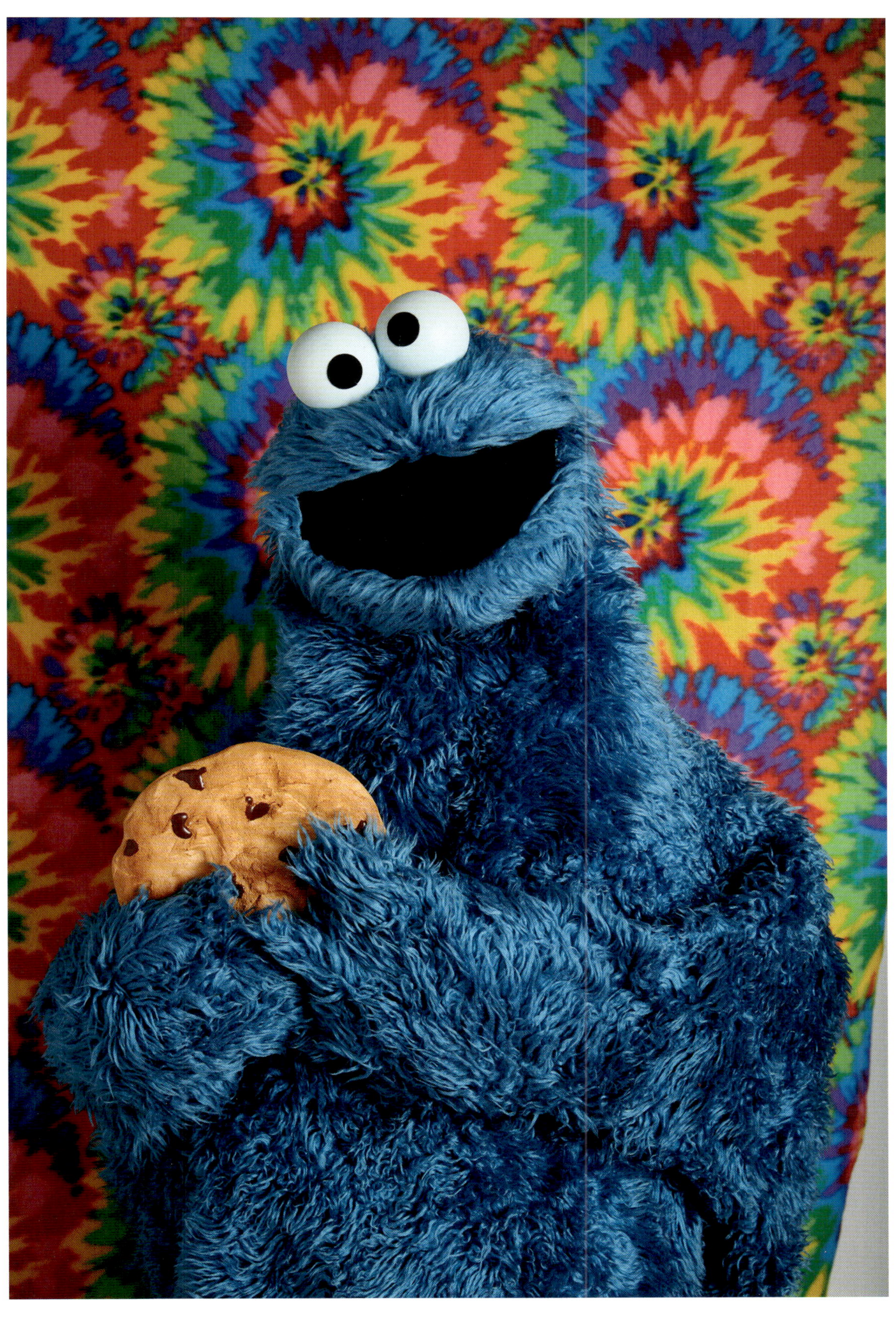

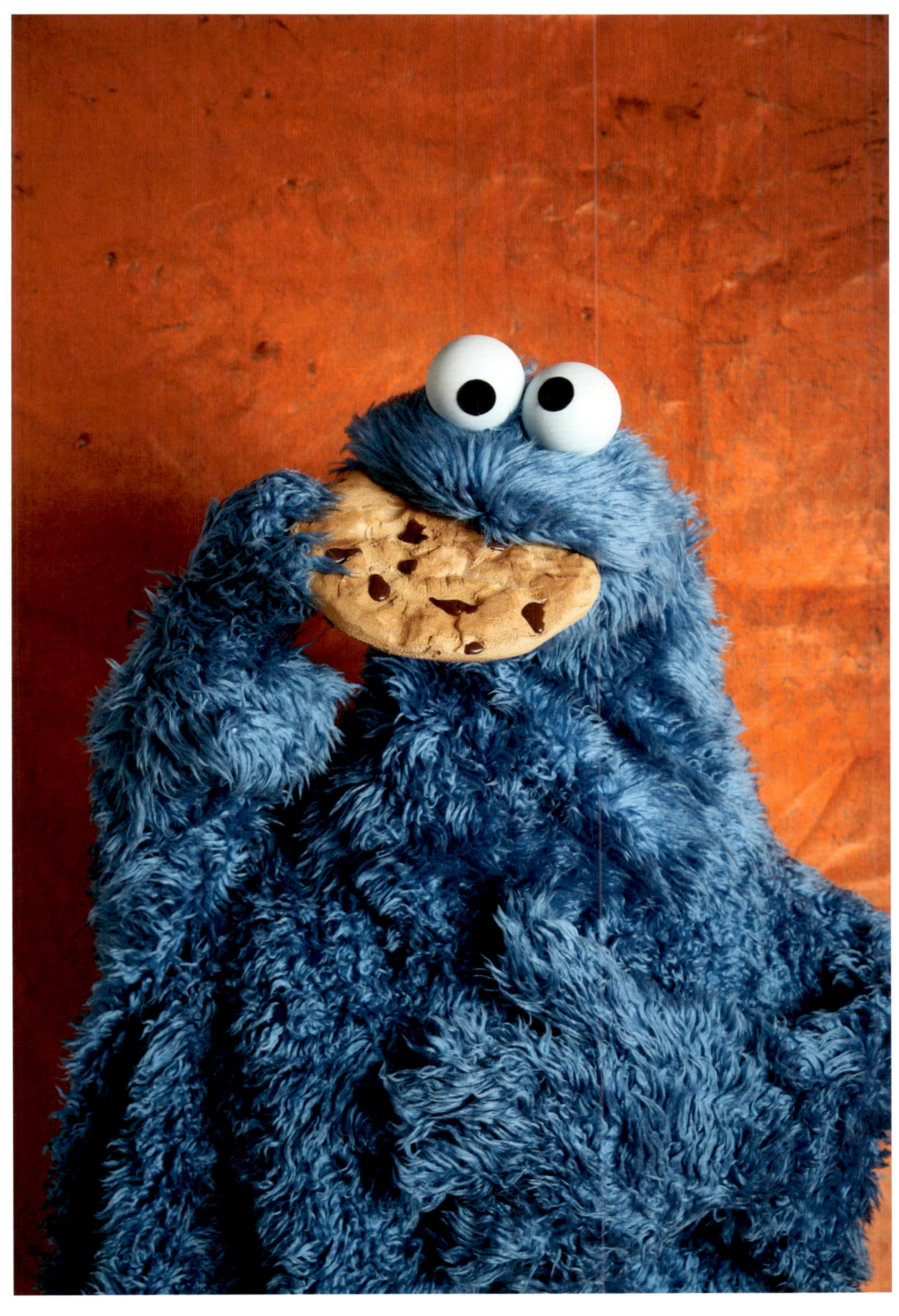

NEBRASKA vs. CLEMSON

1982 ORANGE BOWL

The 48th Annual Classic/January 1, 1982/Three Dollars

SIXTEENTH ANNUAL

PEACH BOWL

Atlanta-Fulton County Stadium
December 30, 1983 $3.00

FLORIDA STATE vs. NORTH CAROLINA

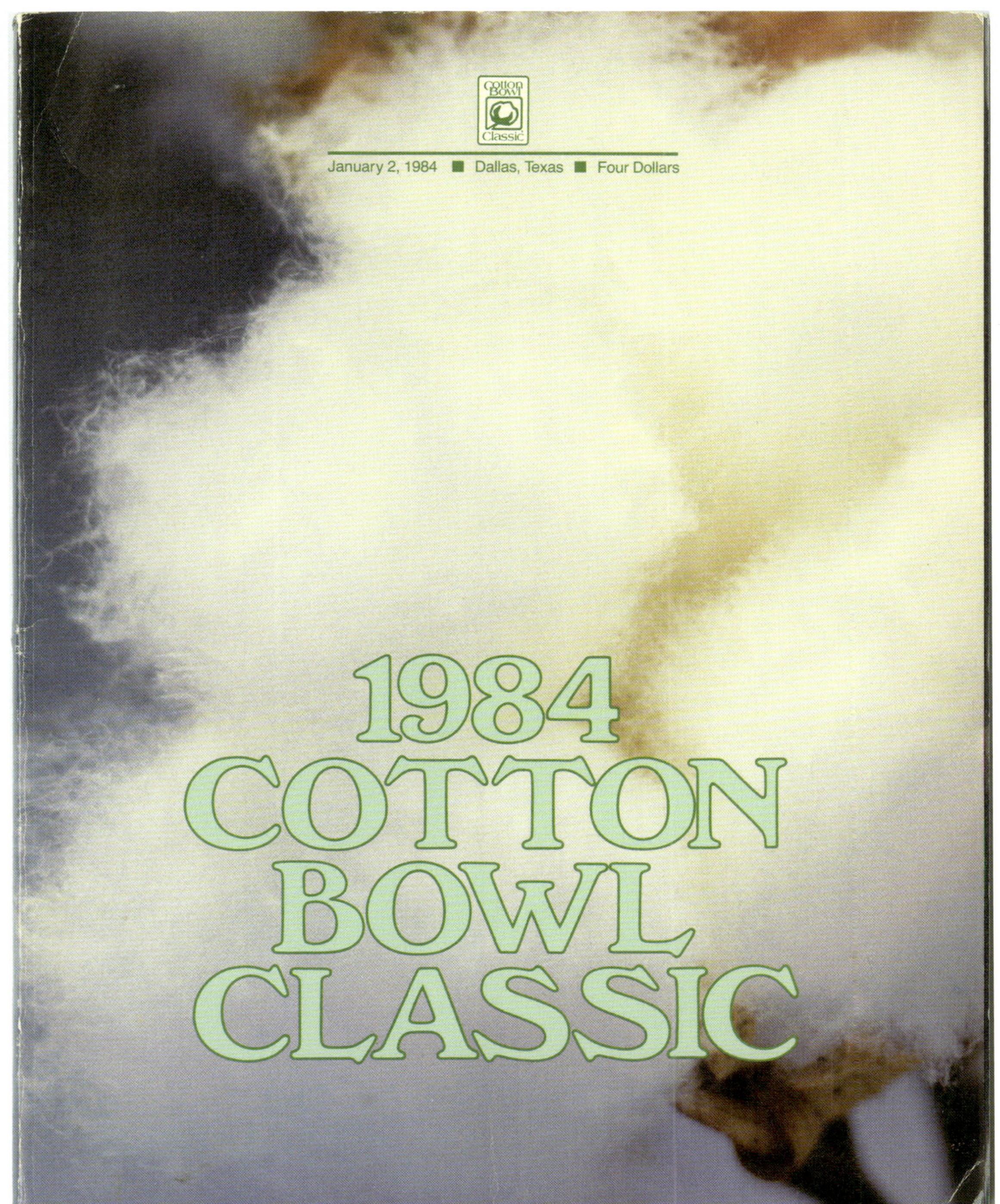
Cotton Bowl Classic
January 2, 1984 ■ Dallas, Texas ■ Four Dollars
1984
COTTON
BOWL
CLASSIC

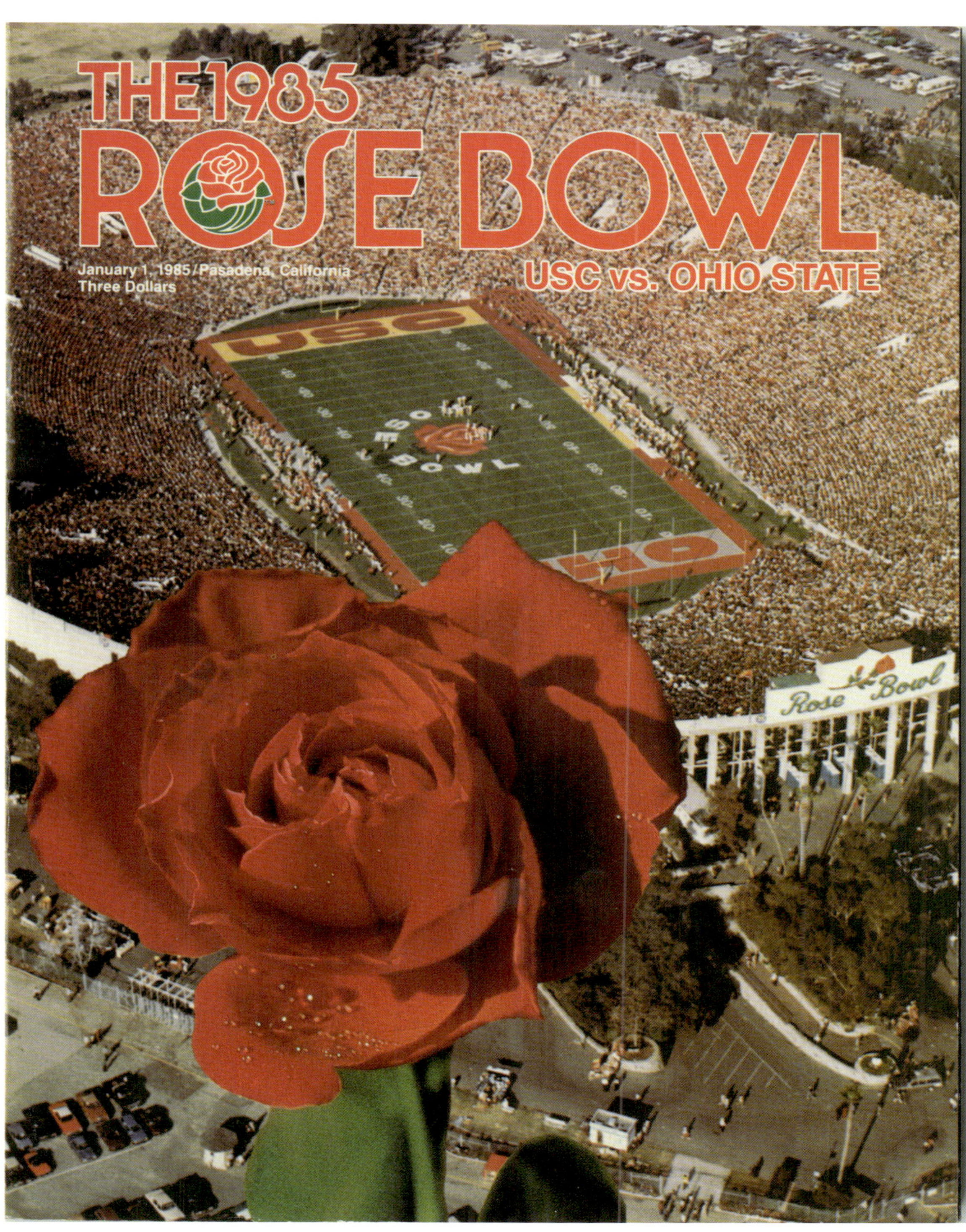
THE 1985
ROSE BOWL
January 1, 1985/Pasadena, California
Three Dollars
USC vs. OHIO STATE
USC
ROSE BOWL
OHIO
Rose Bowl

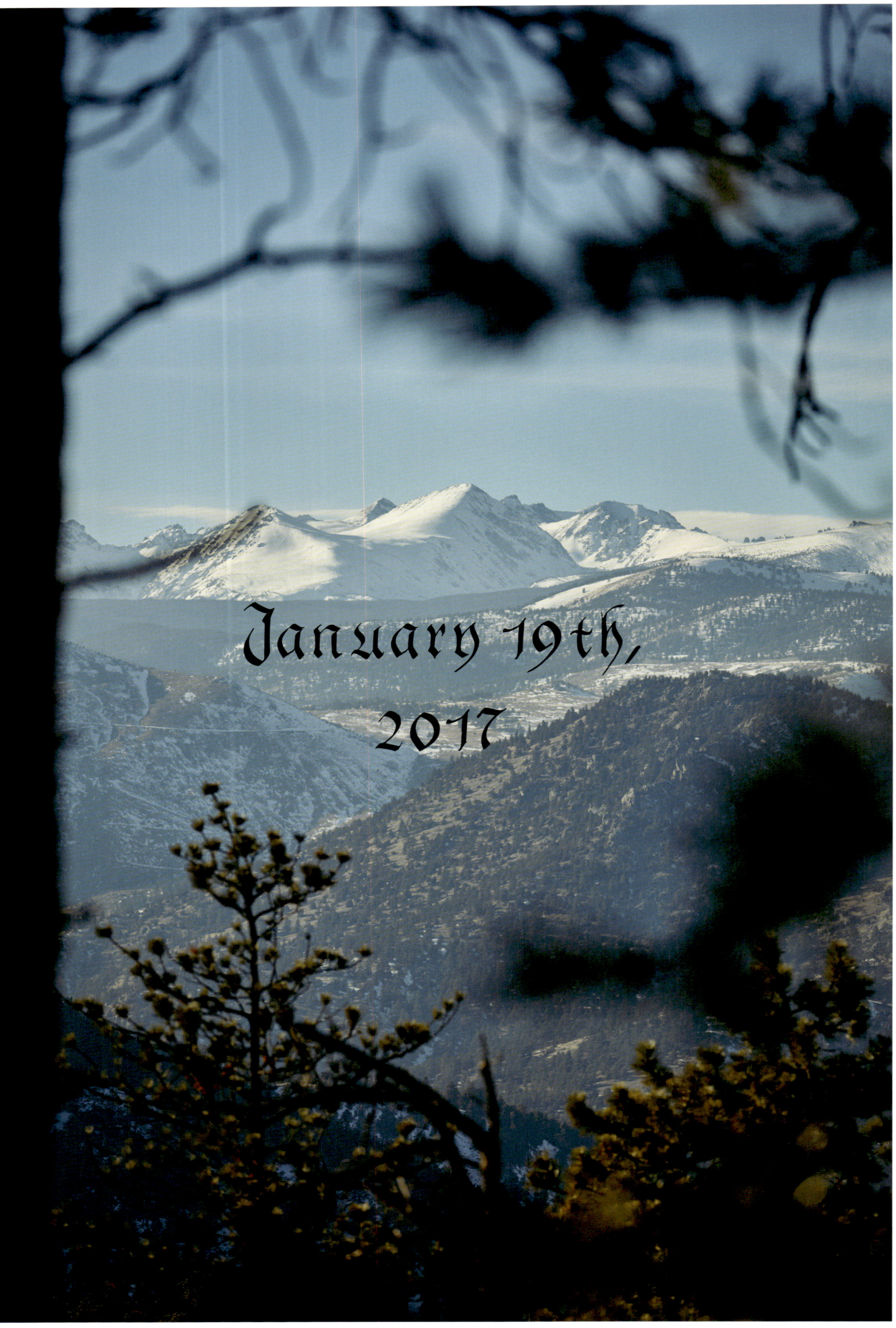
January 19th,
2017

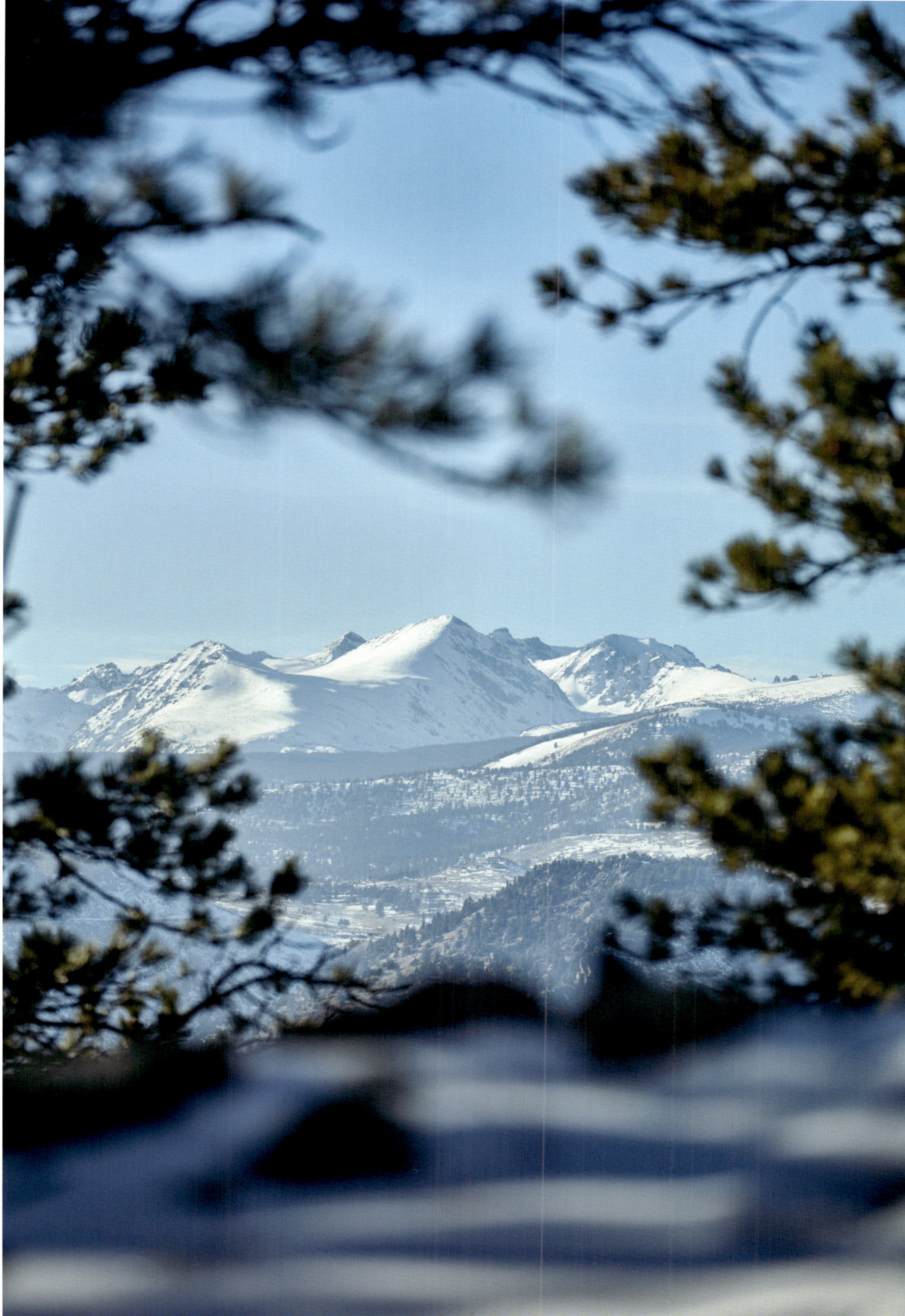

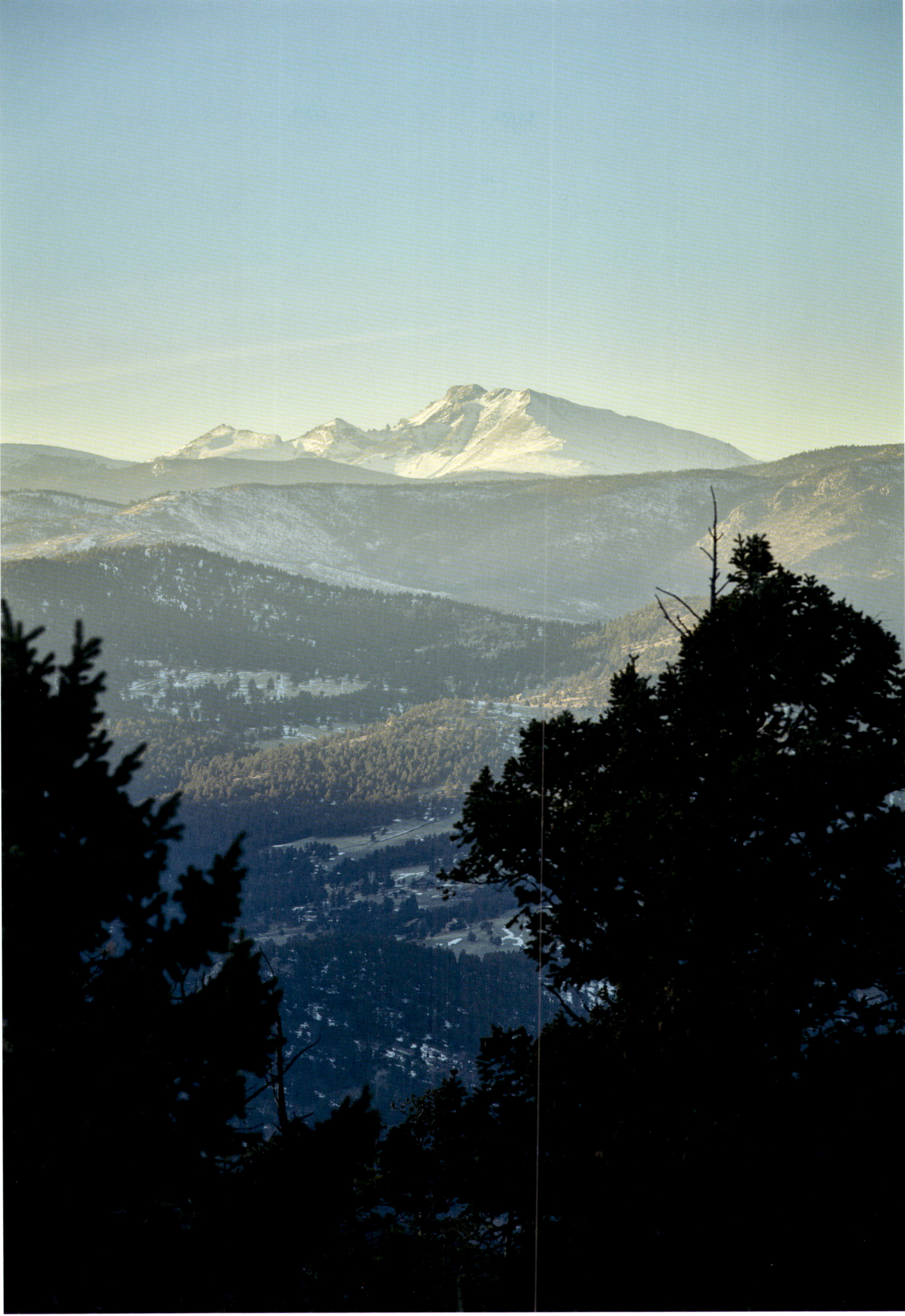

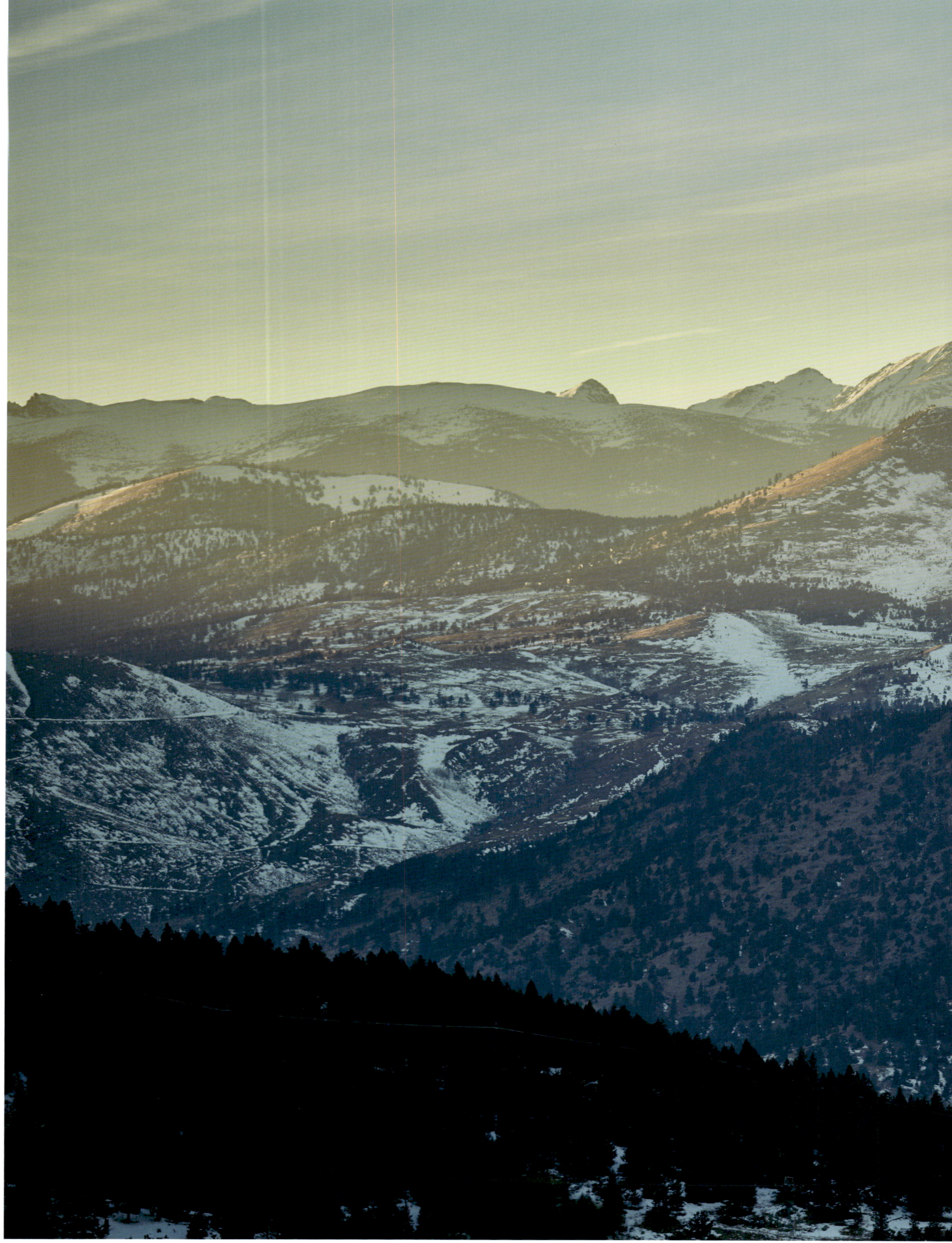

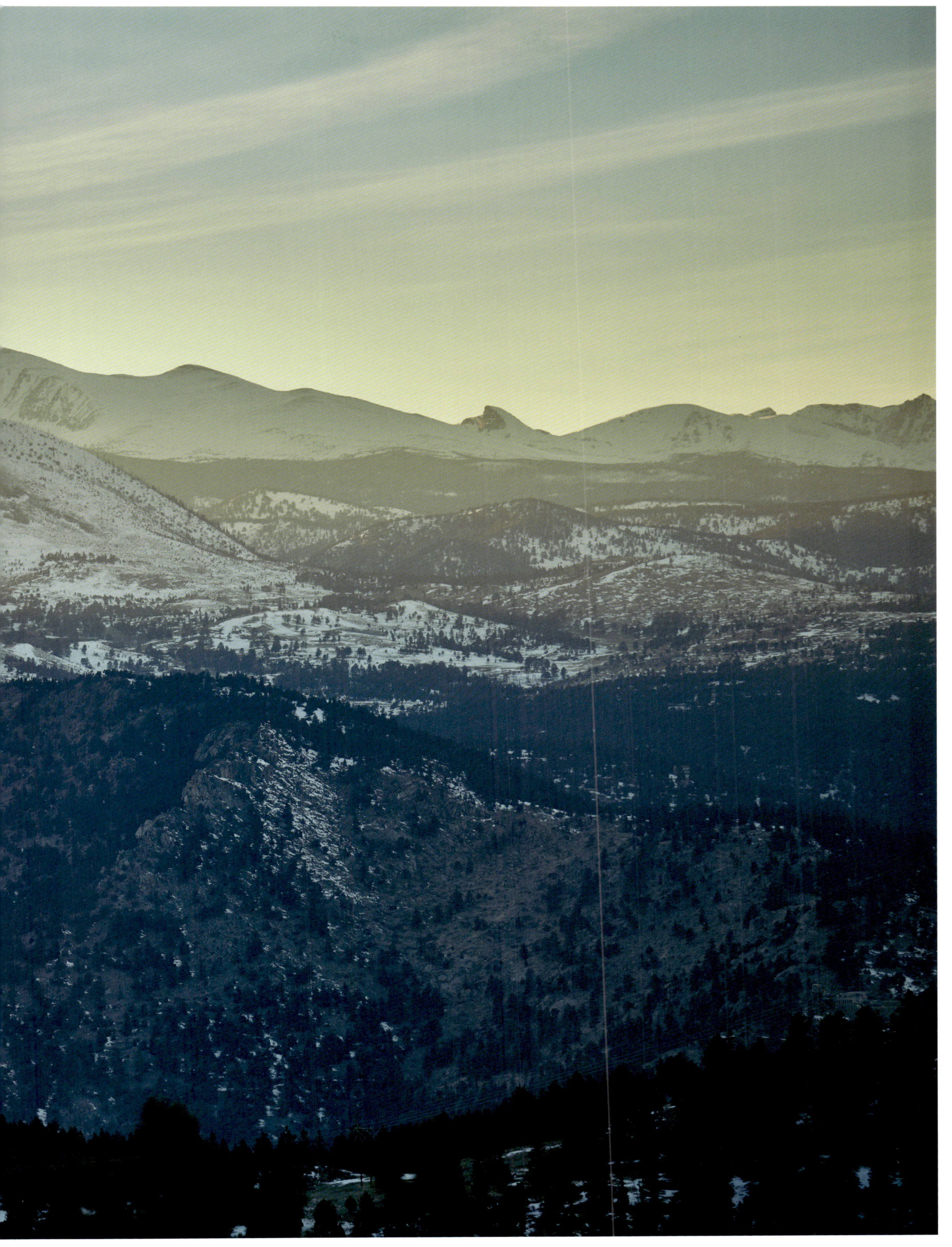

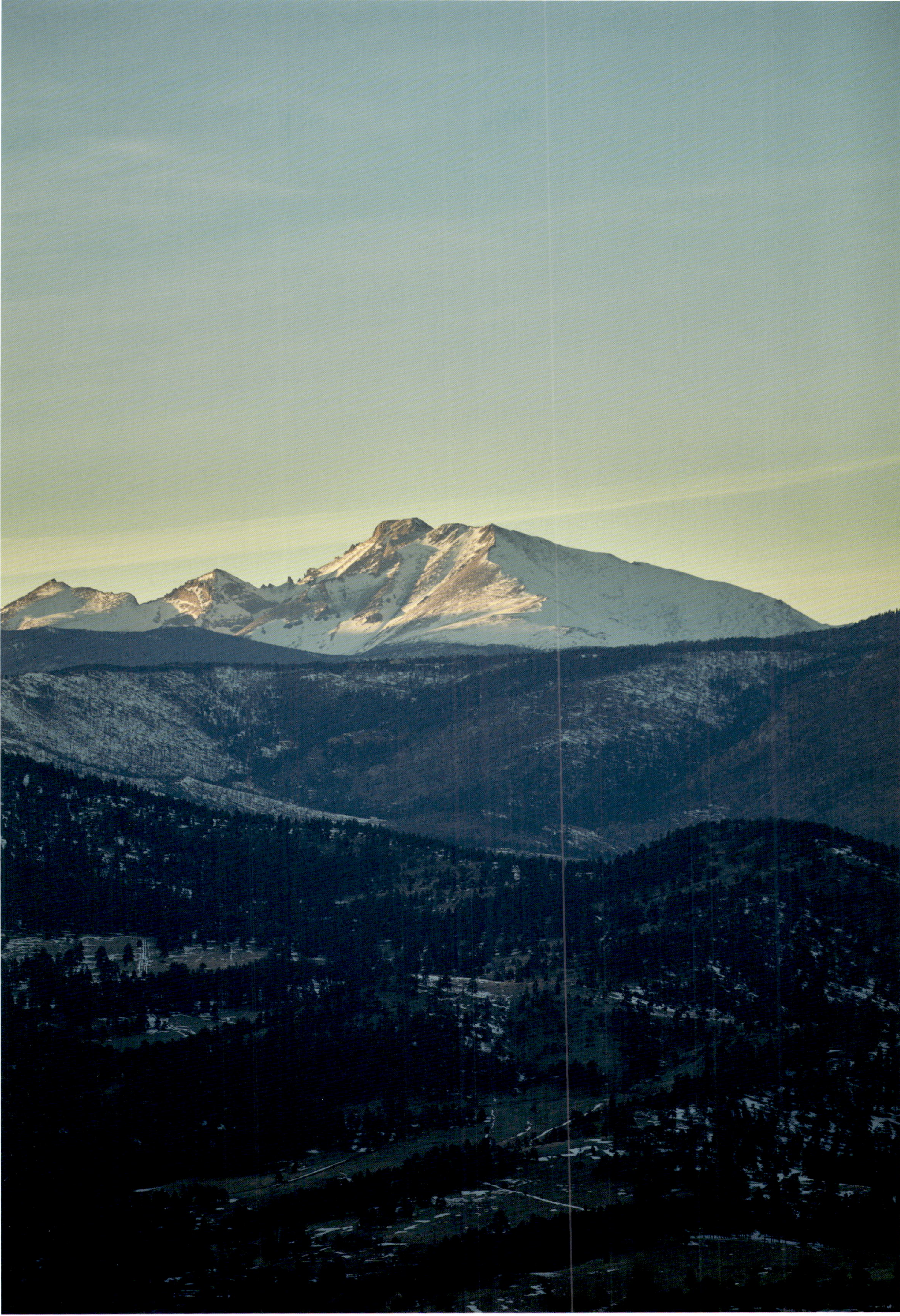

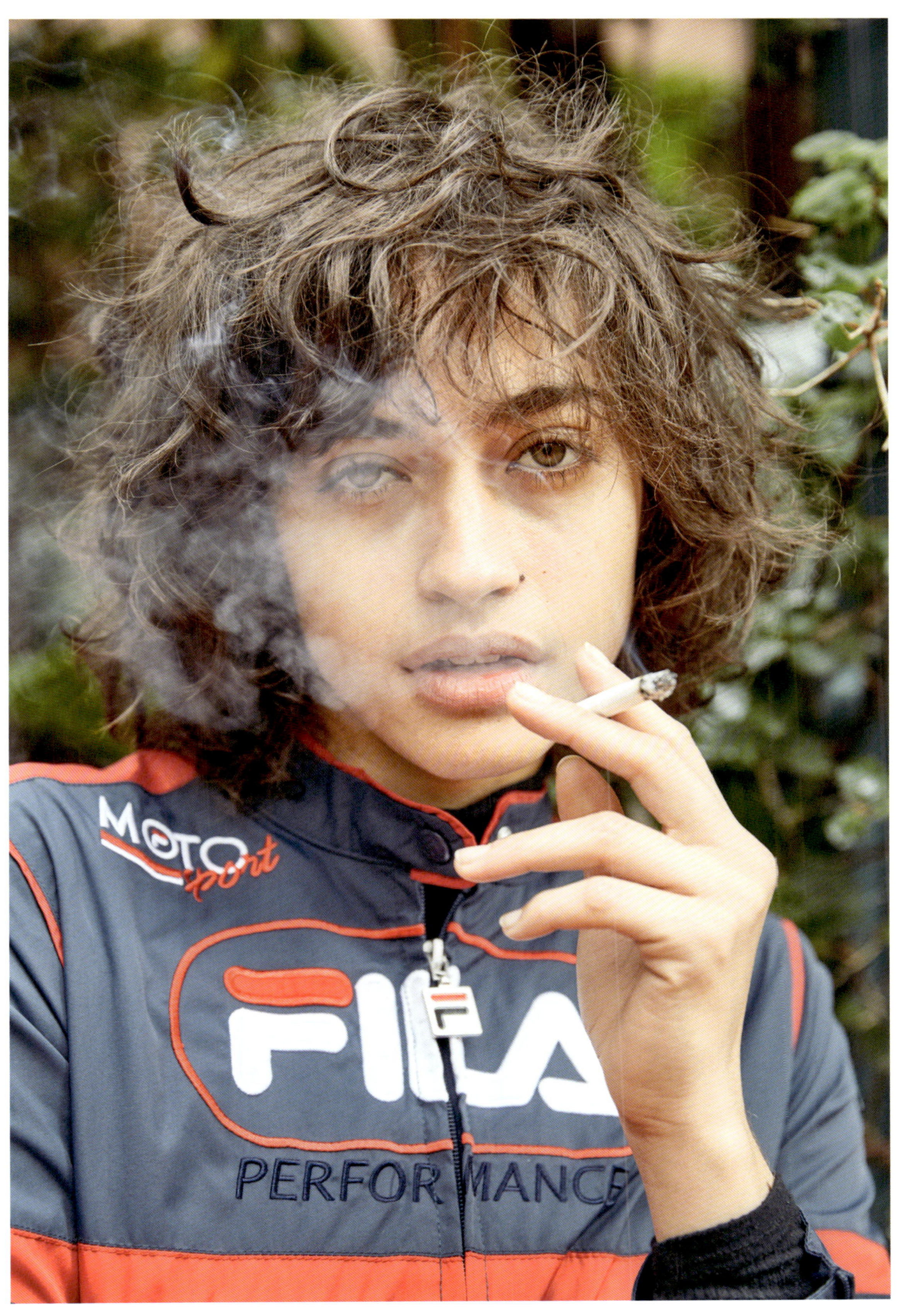
MOTO sport
FILA
PERFORMANCE

January 20th,
2017

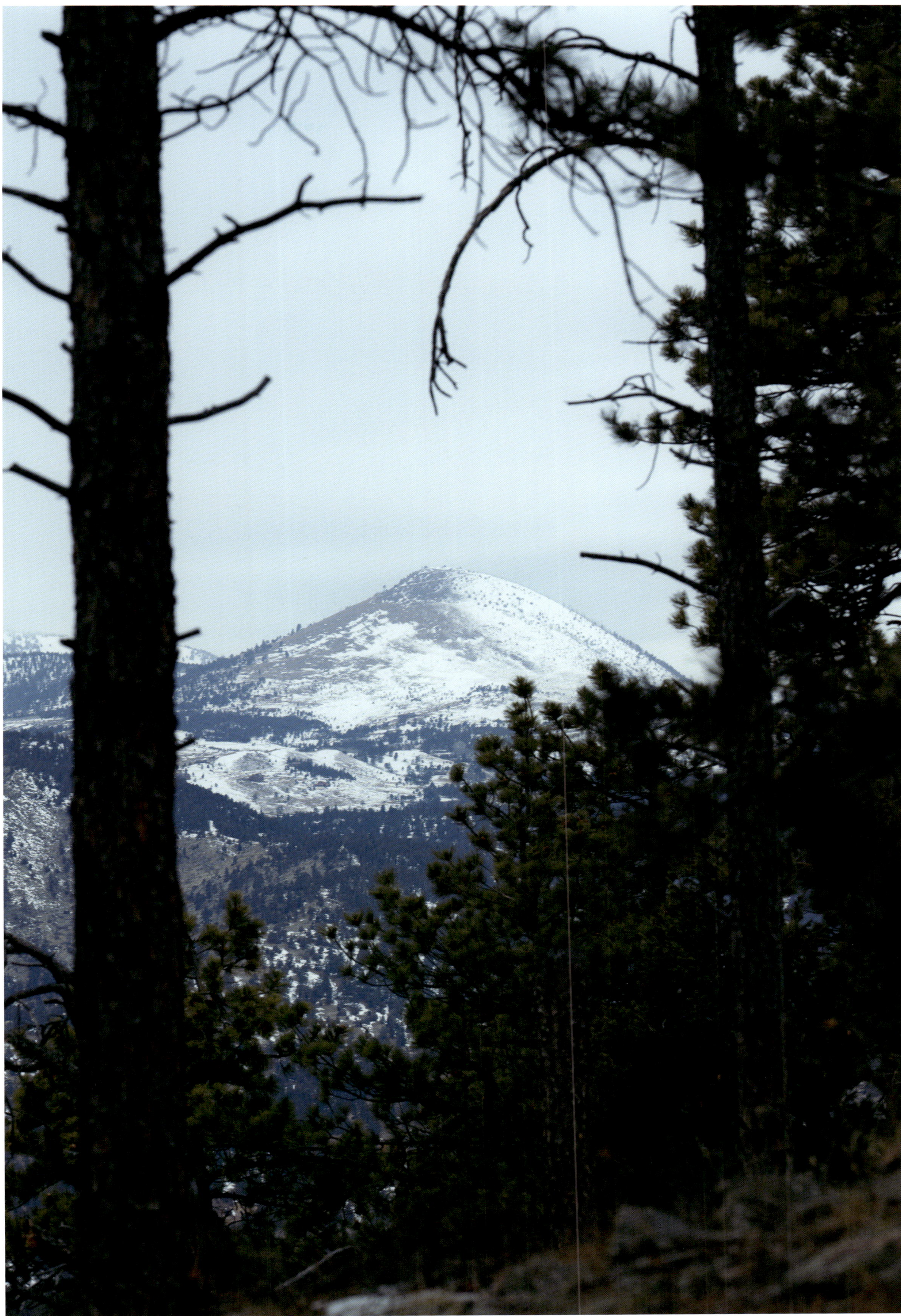

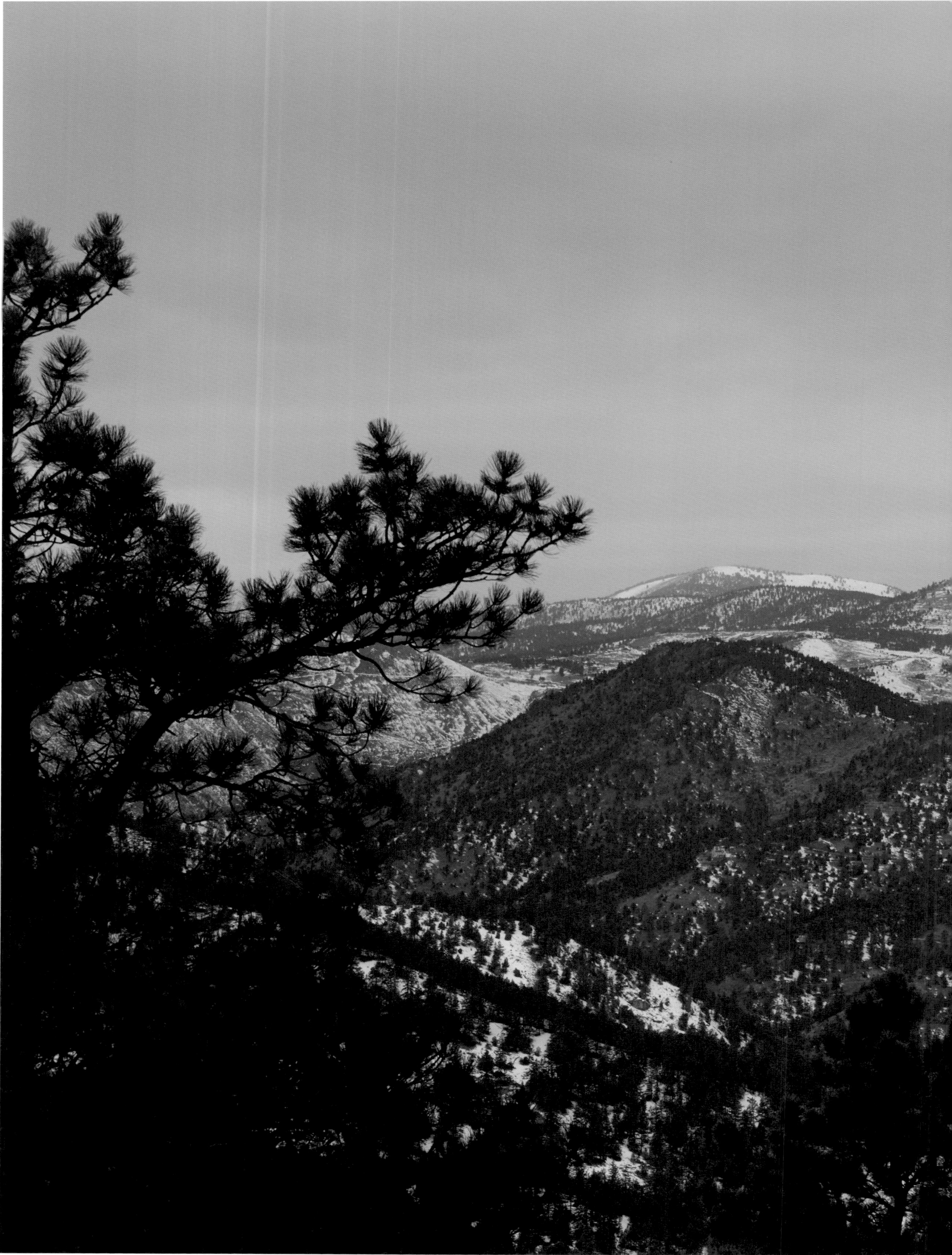

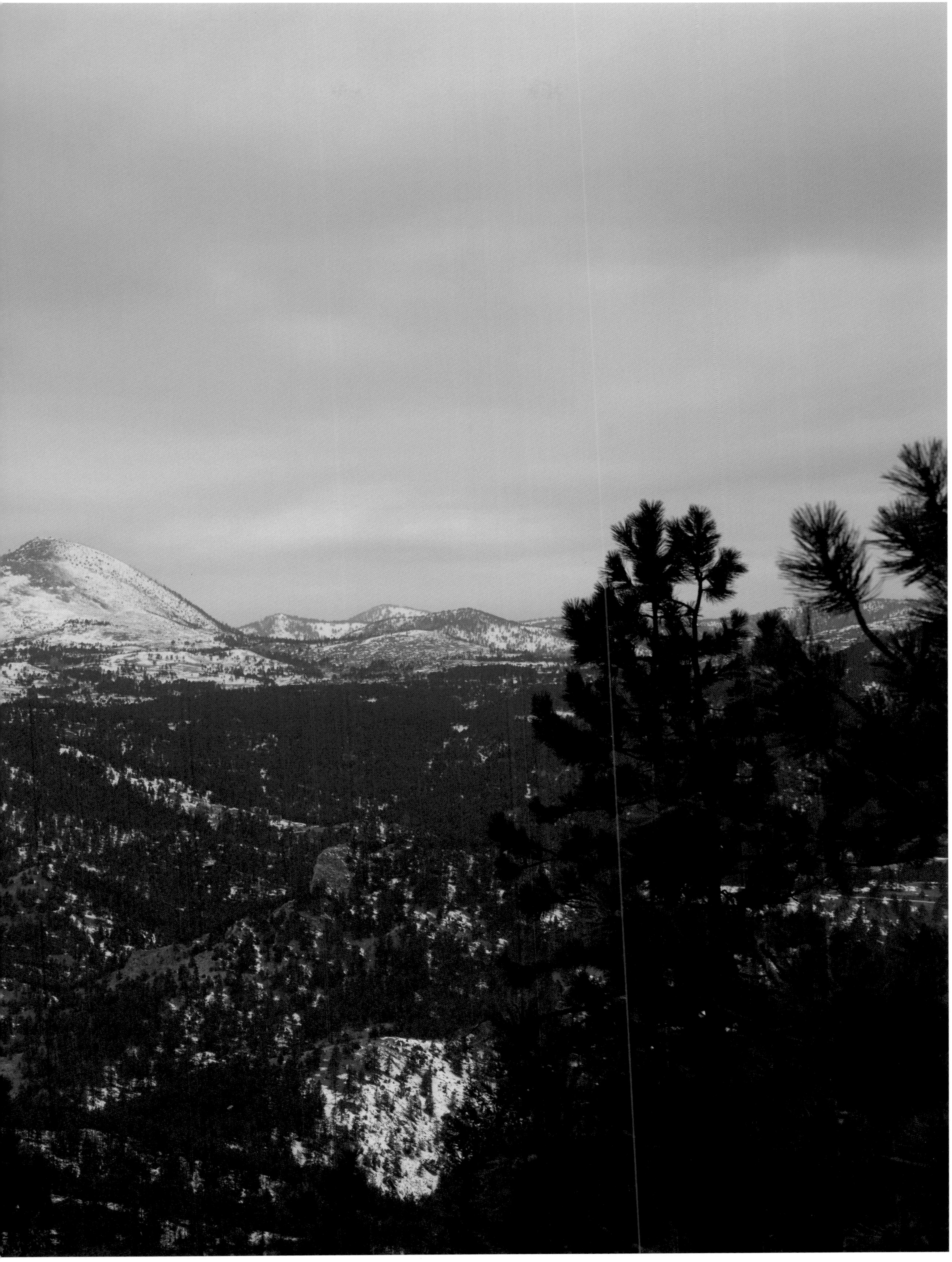

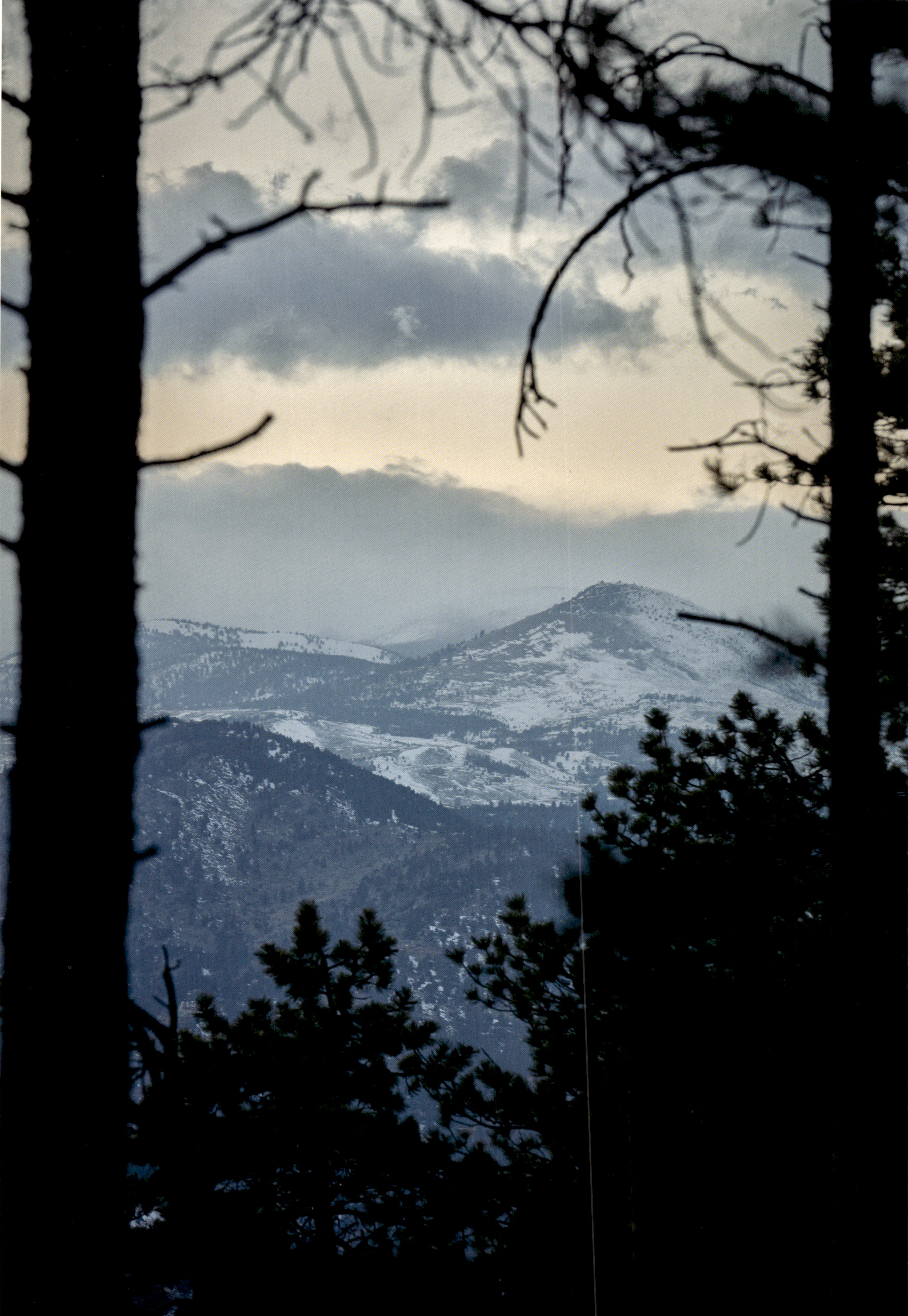

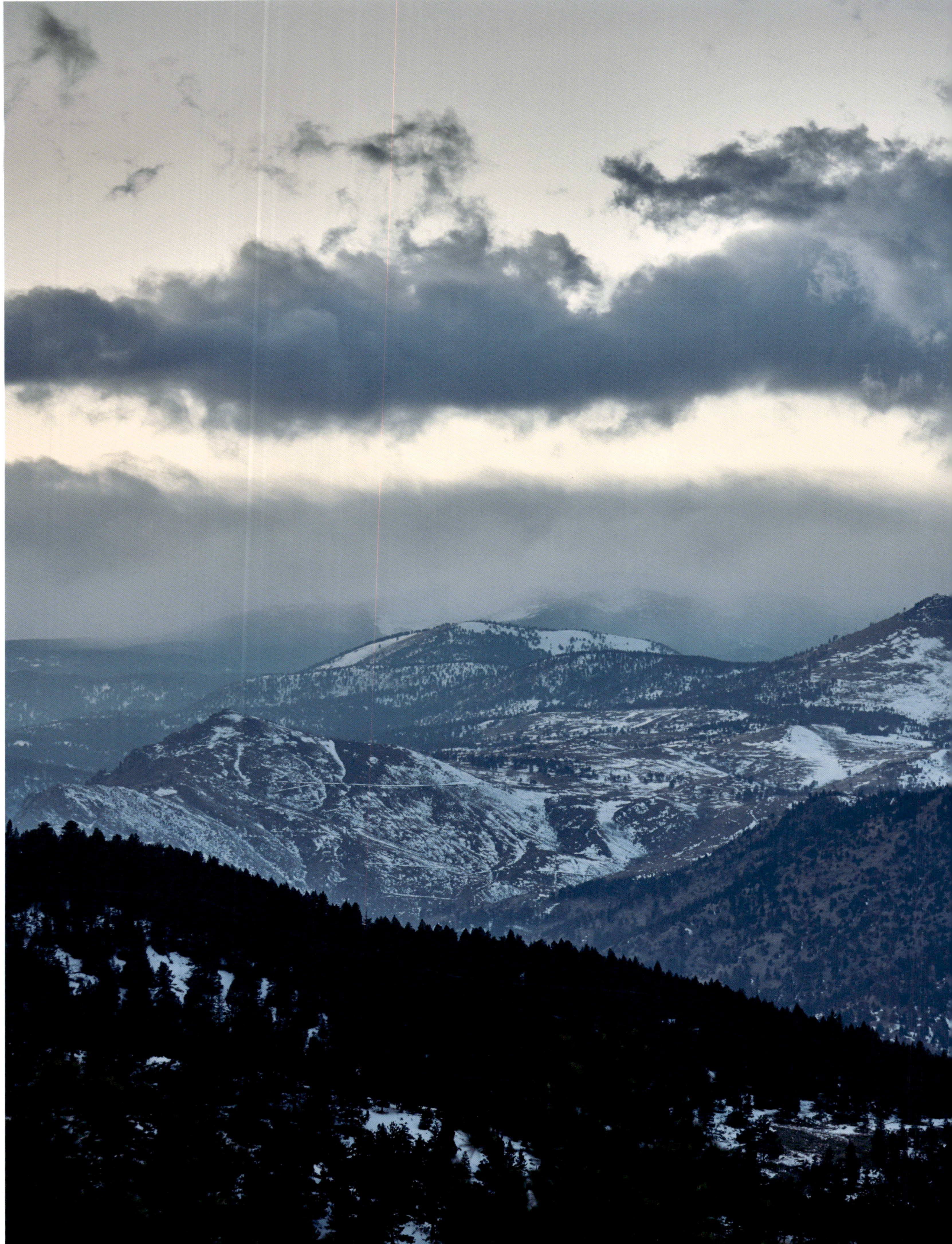

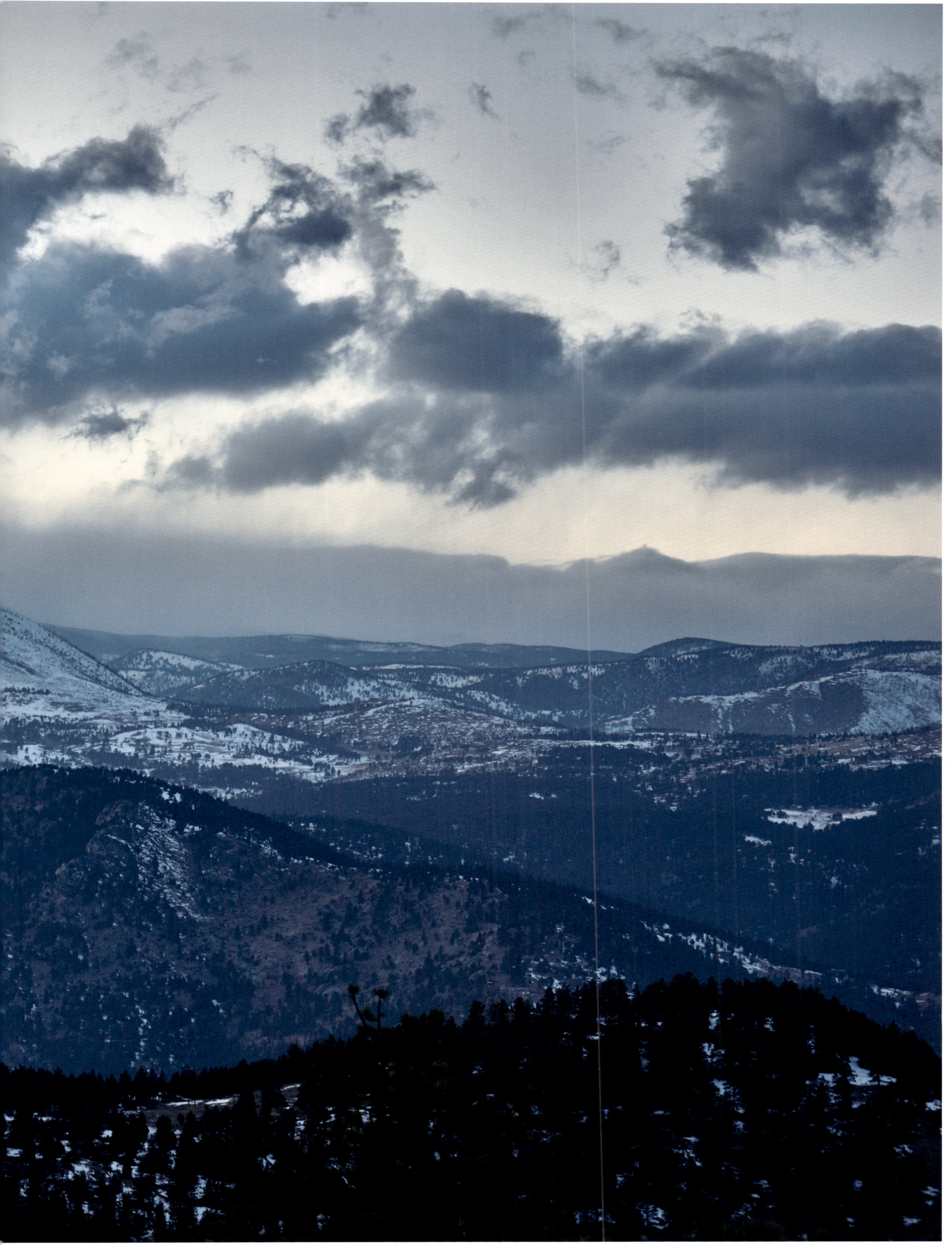

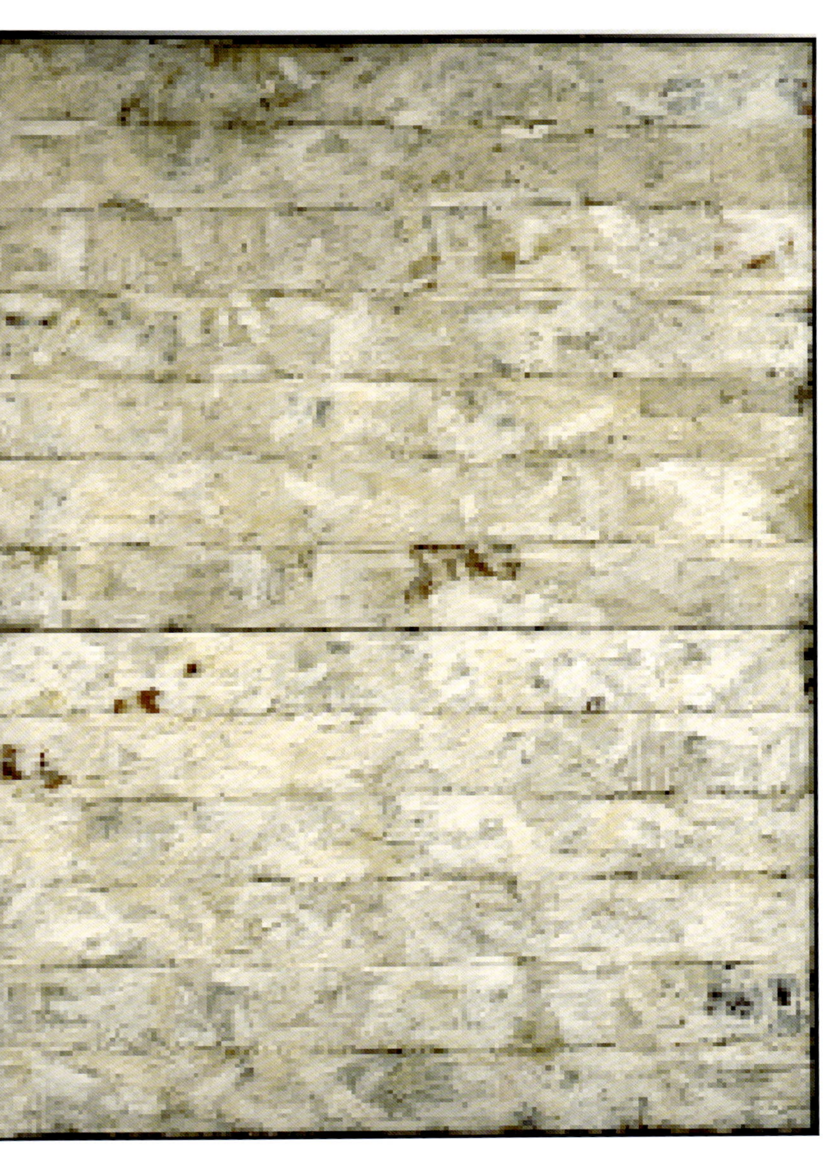

January 21st,
2017

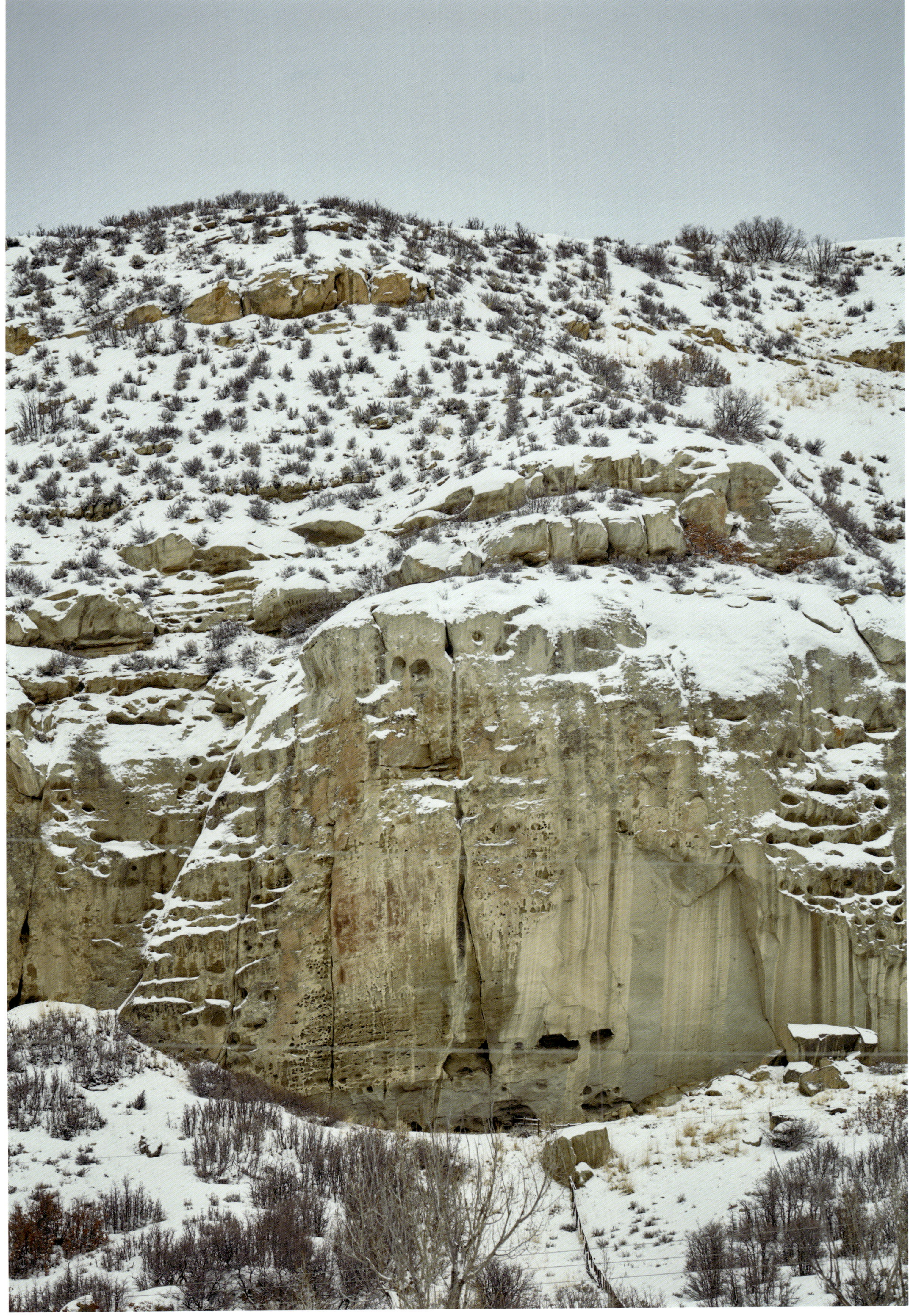

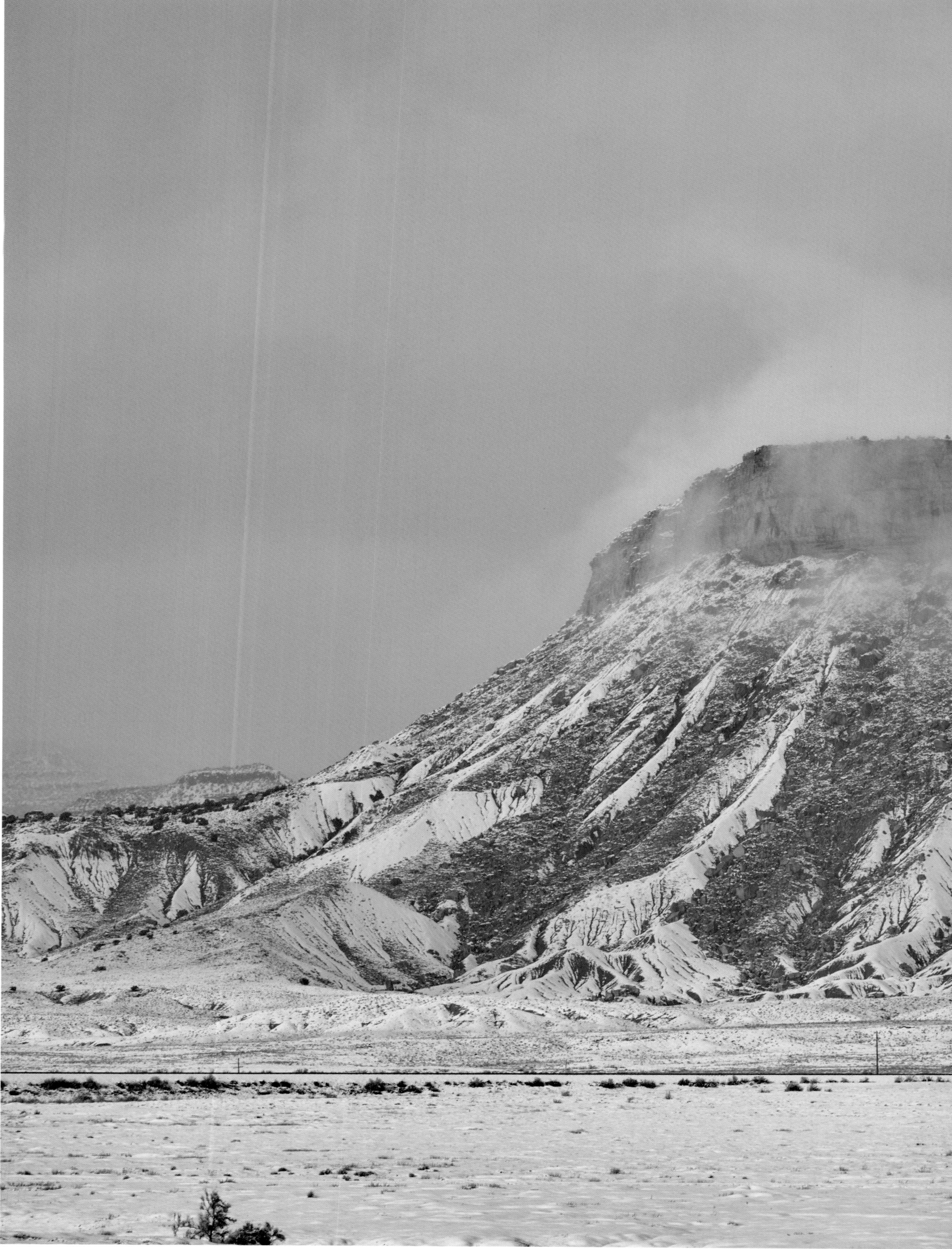

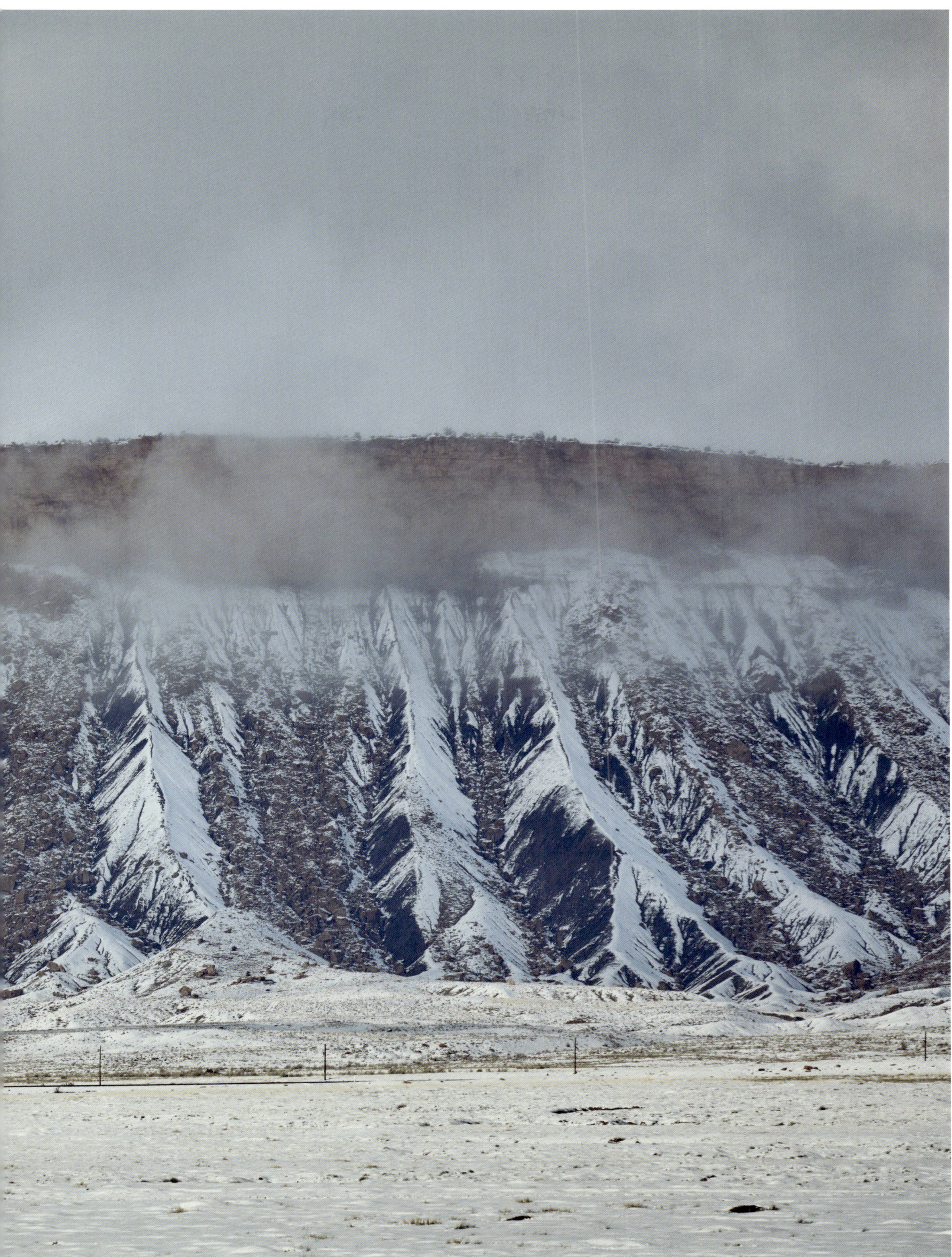

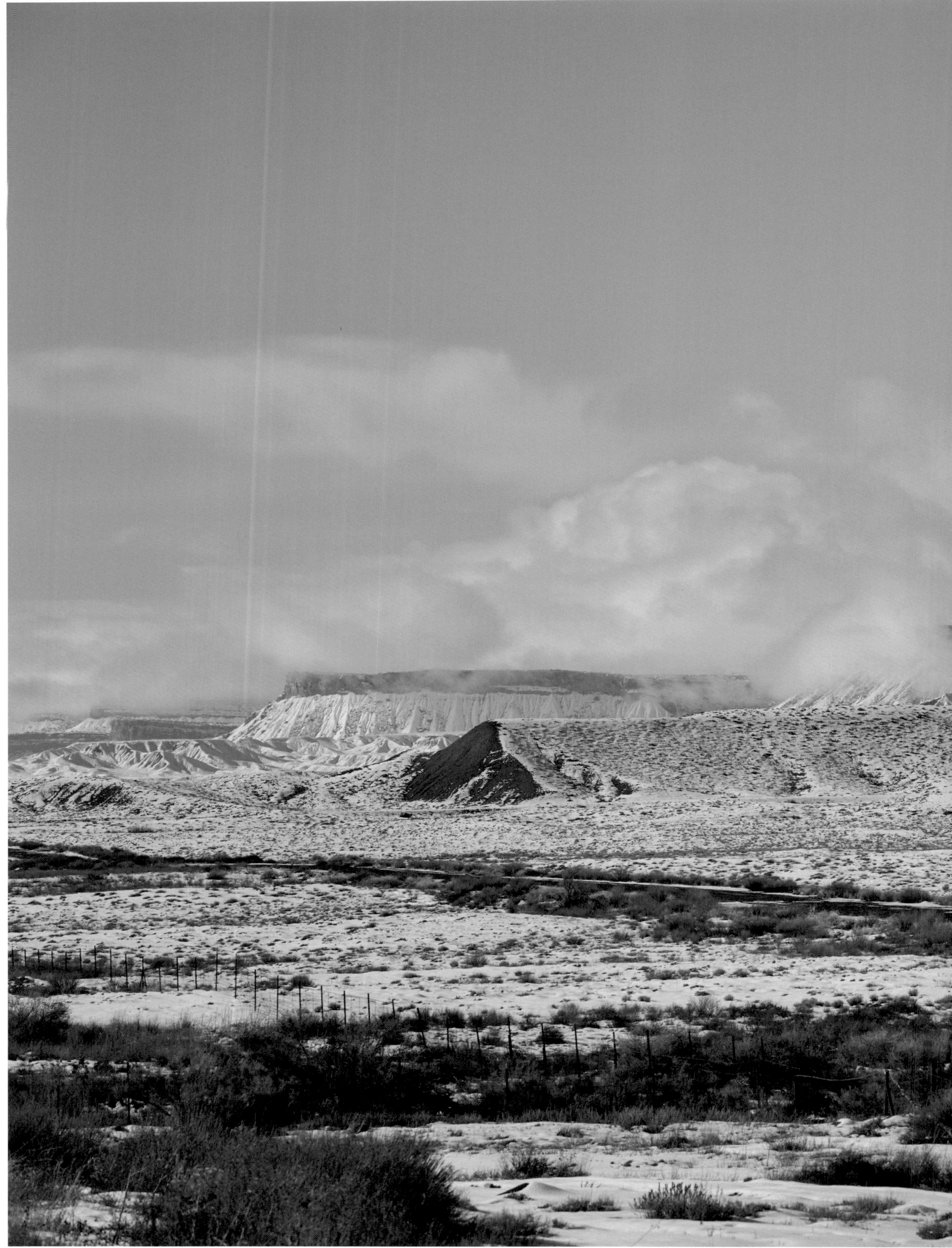

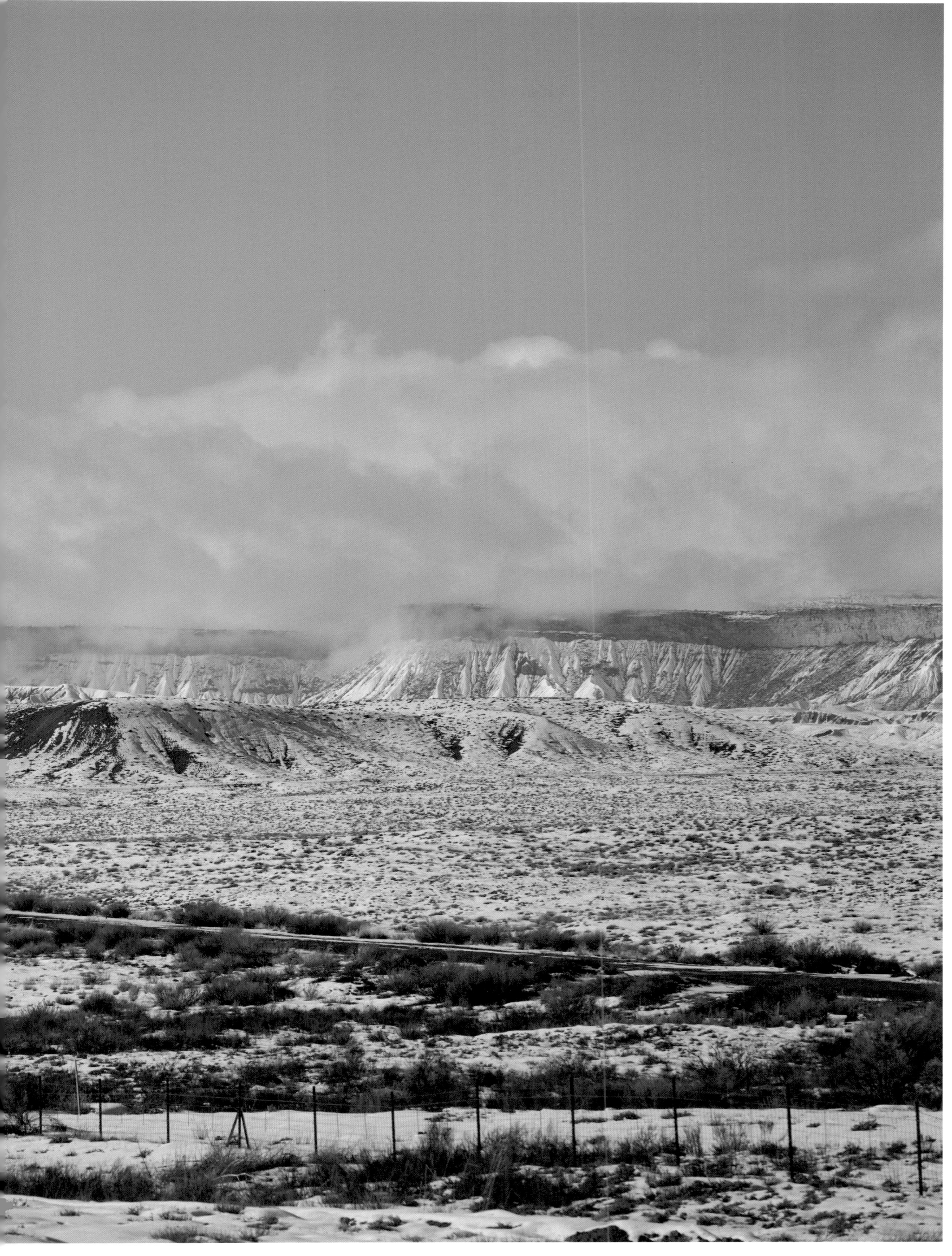

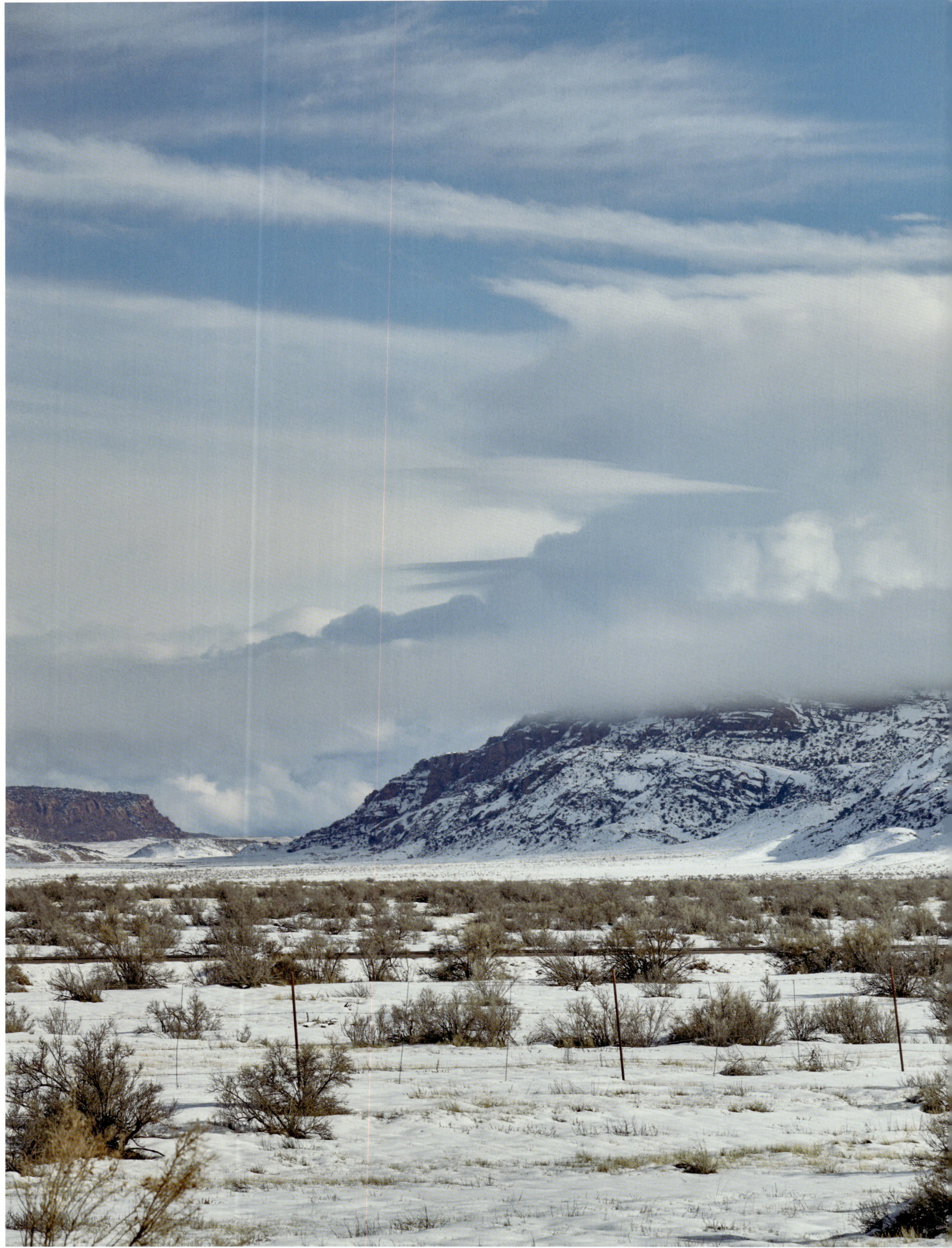

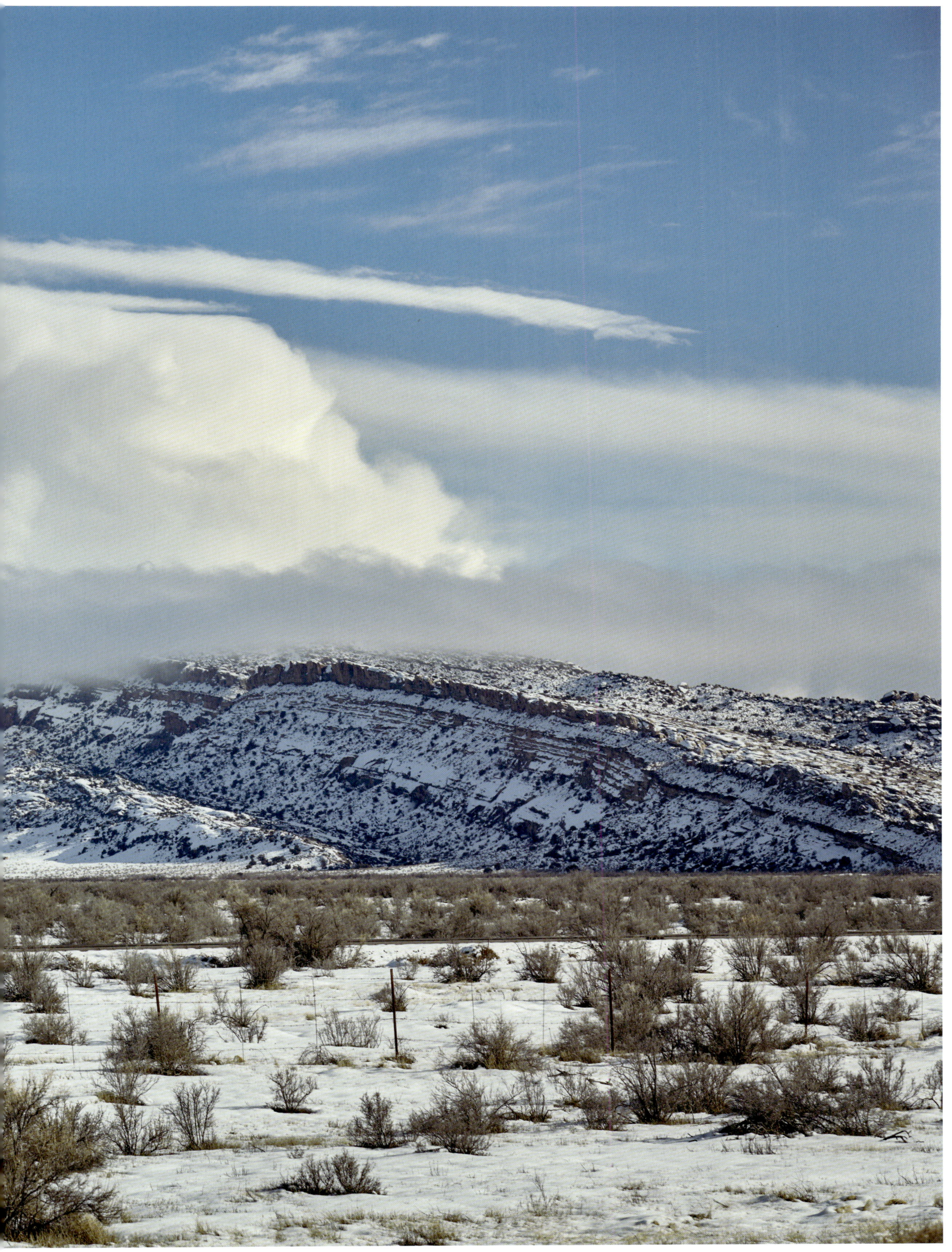

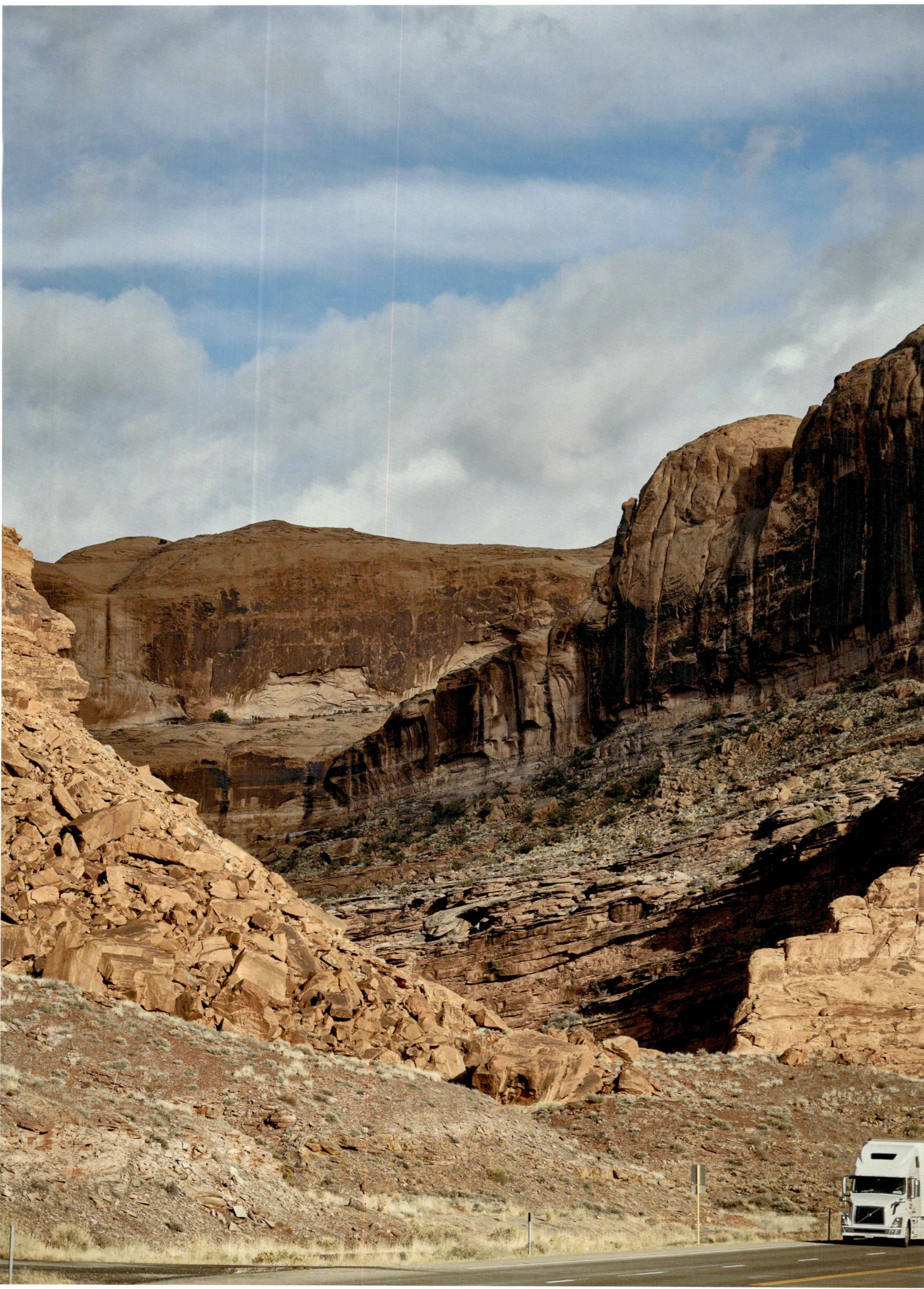

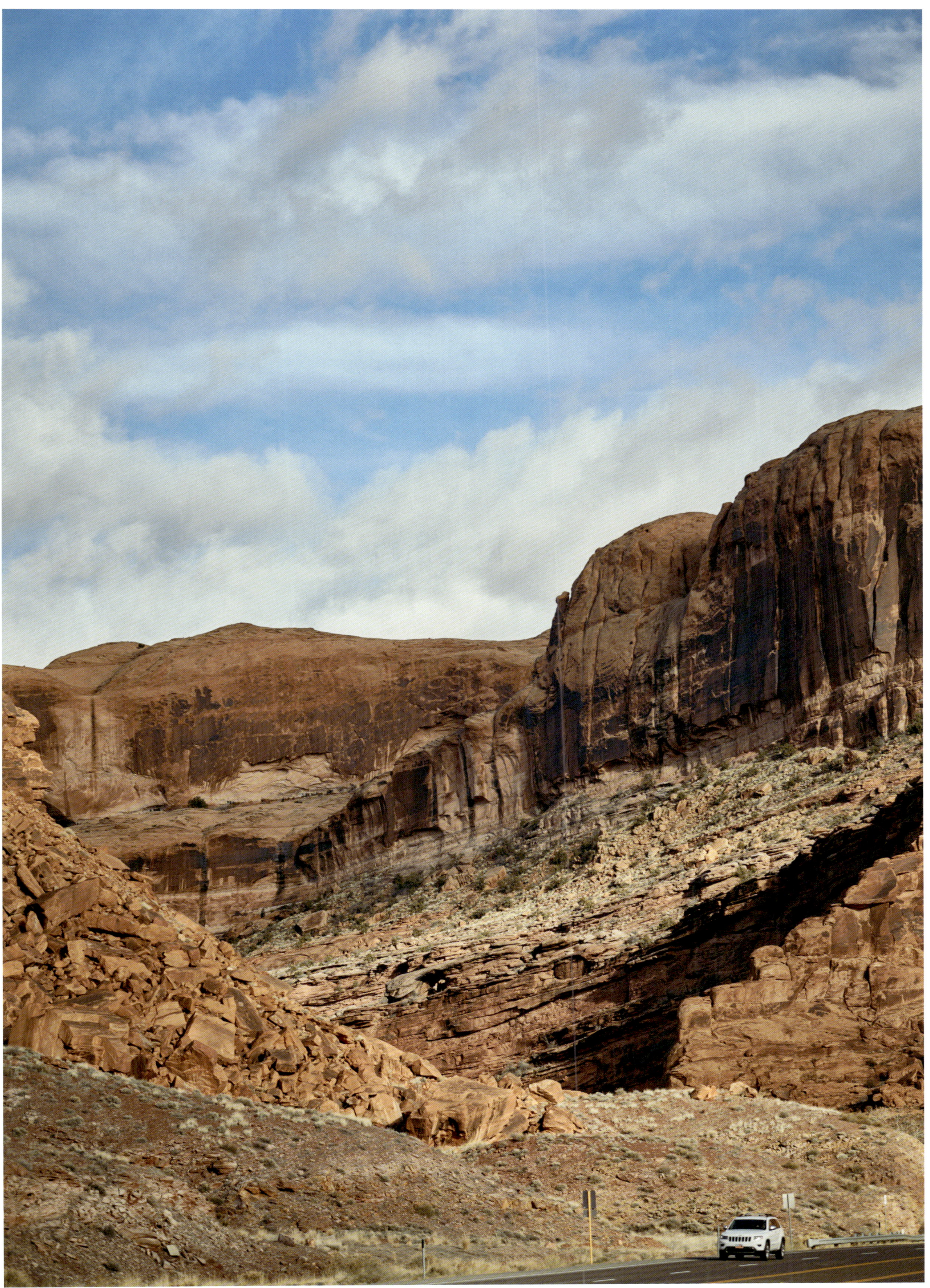

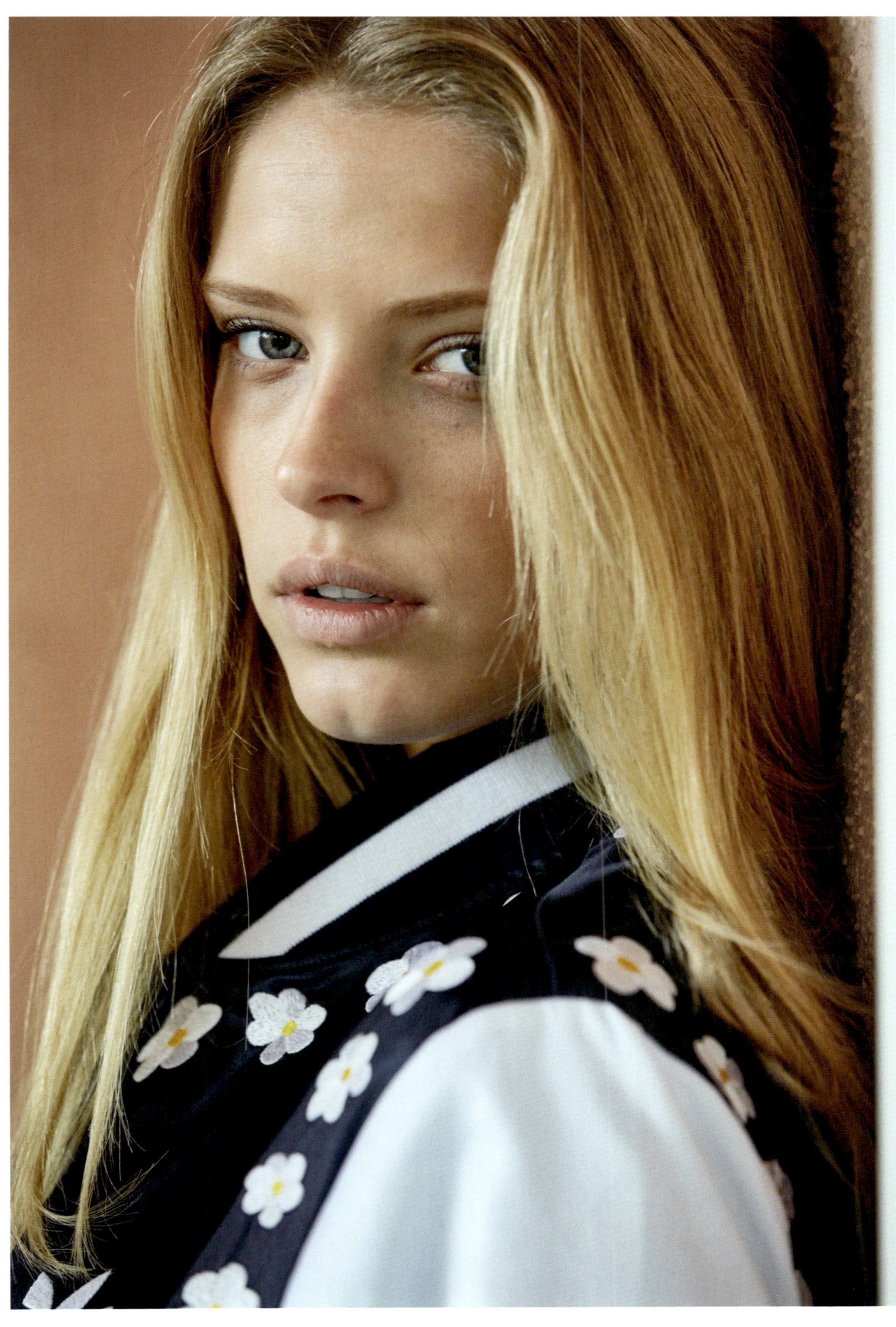

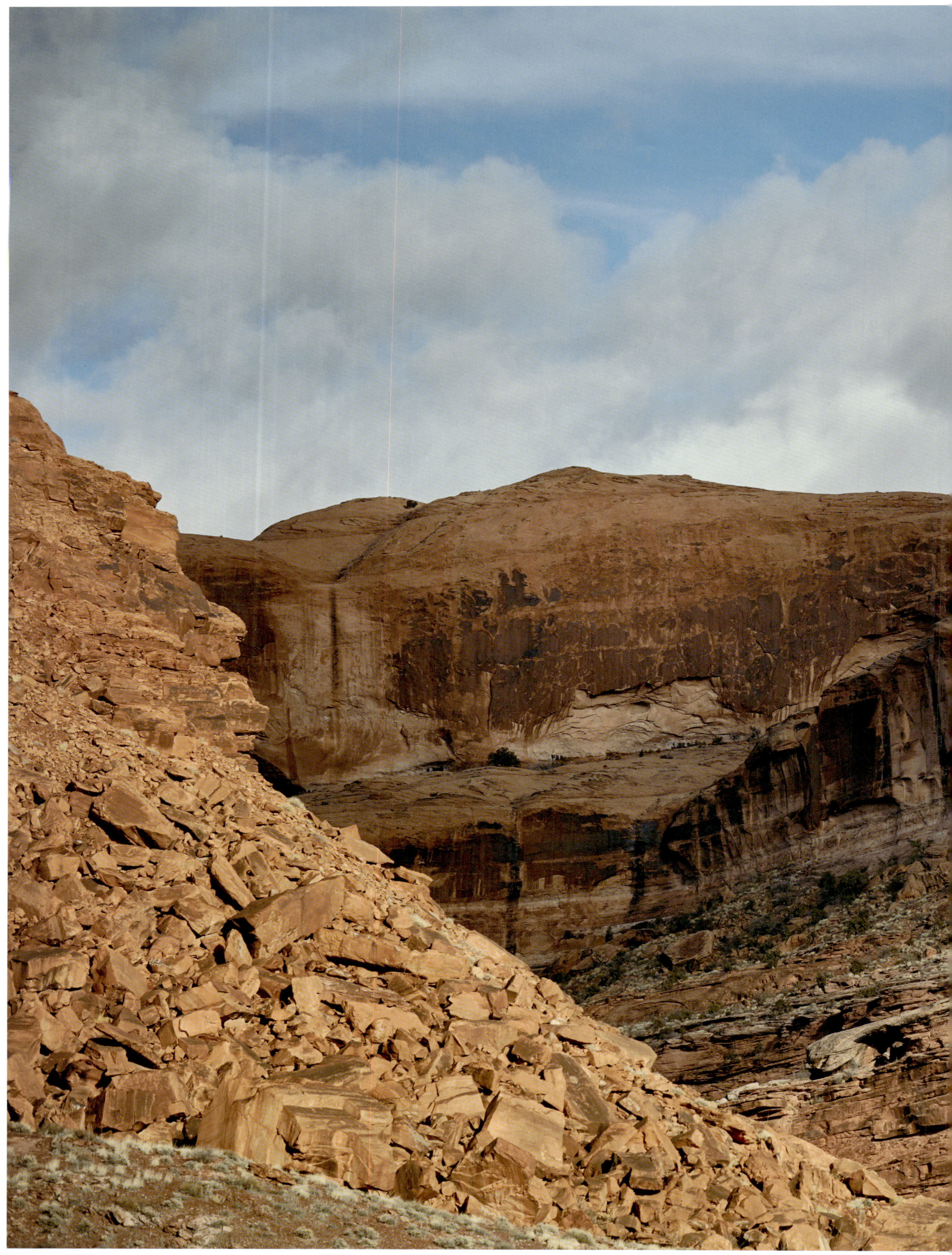

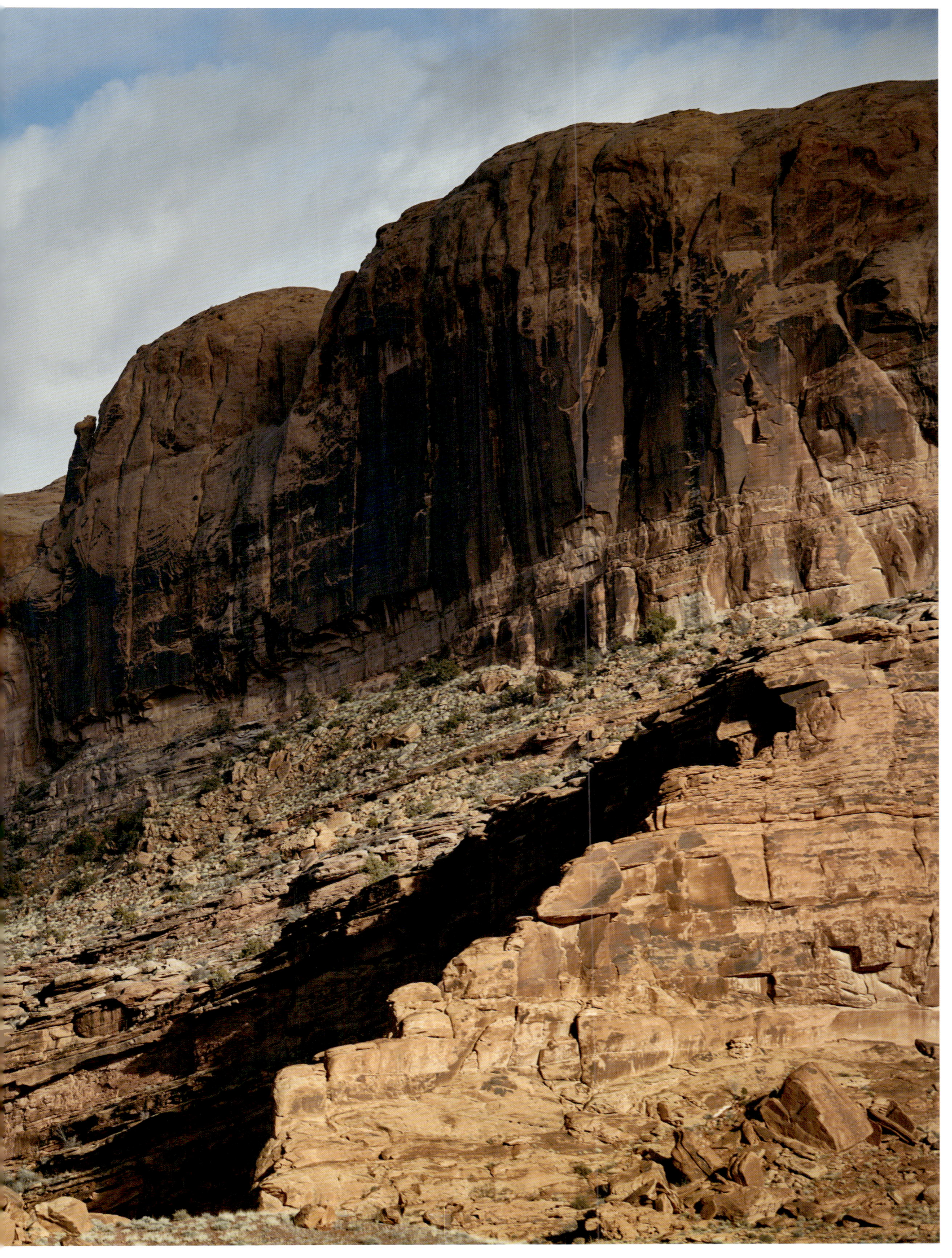

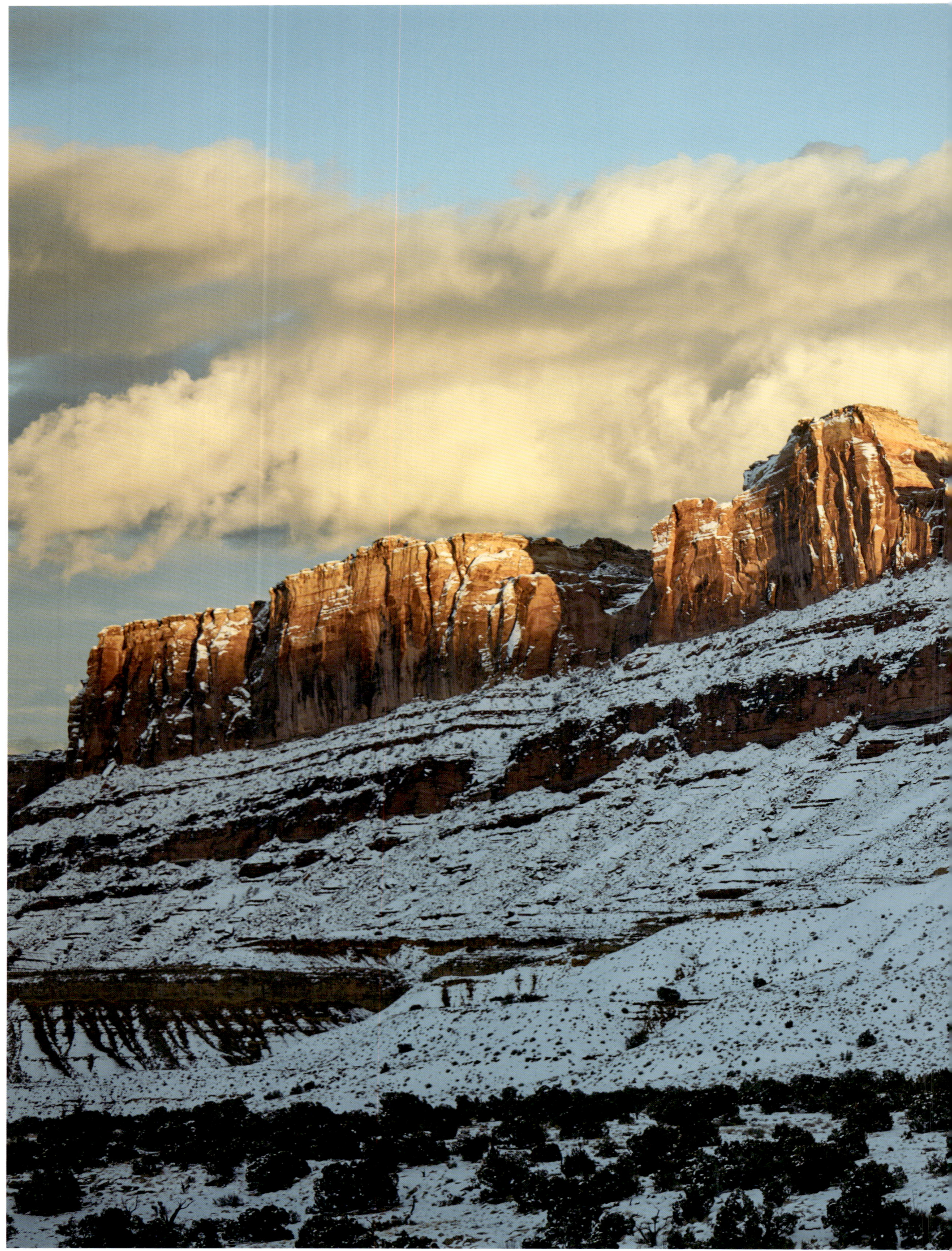

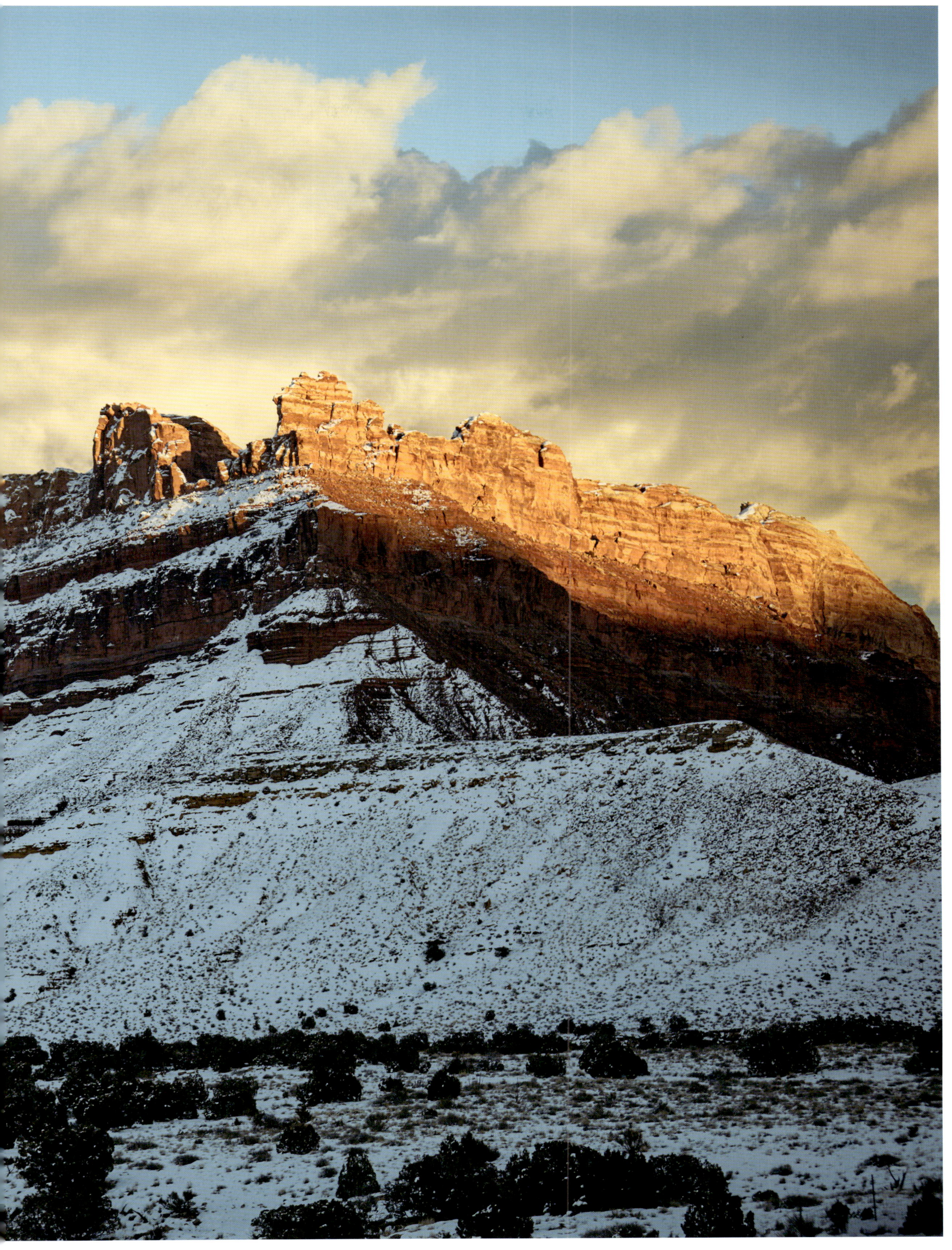

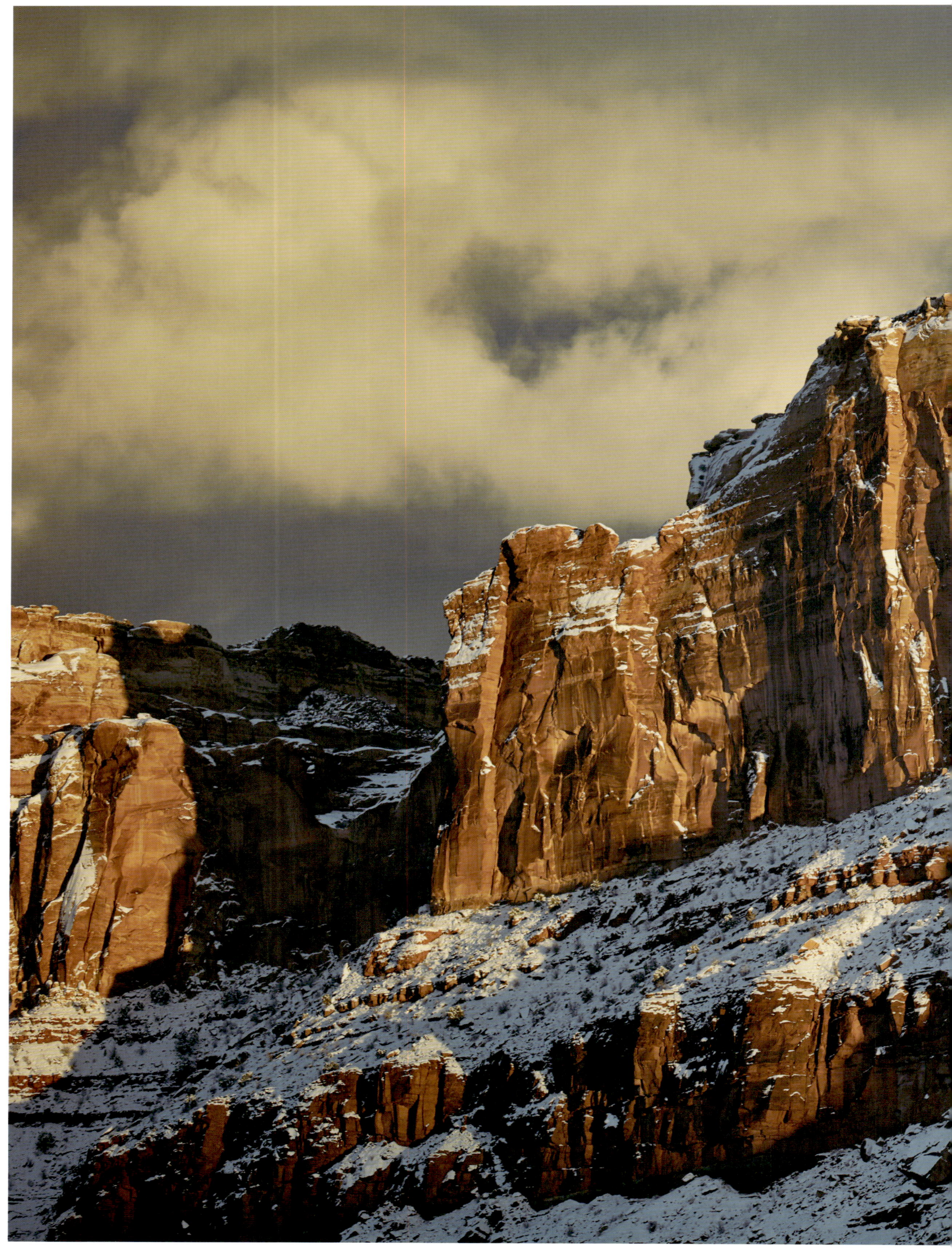

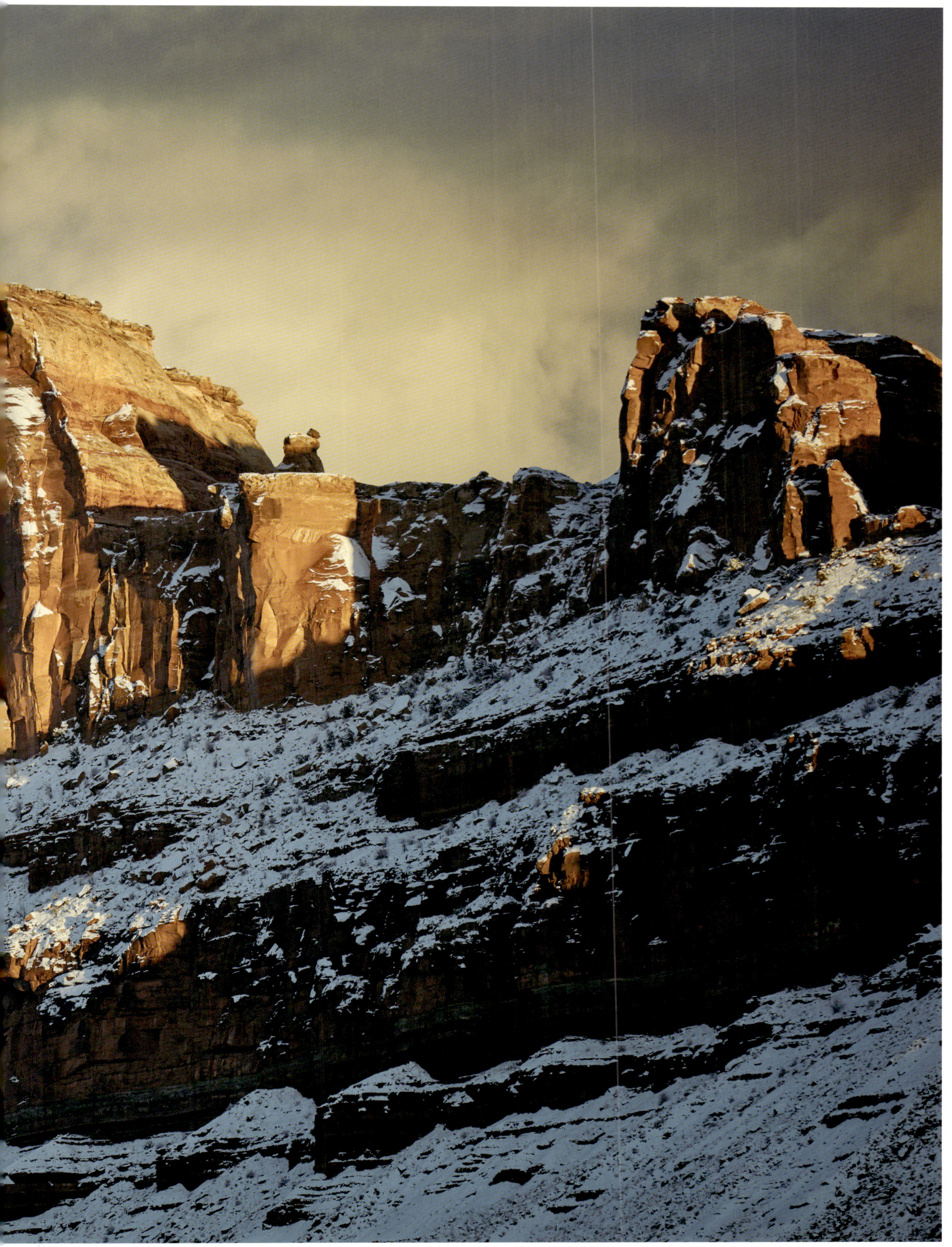

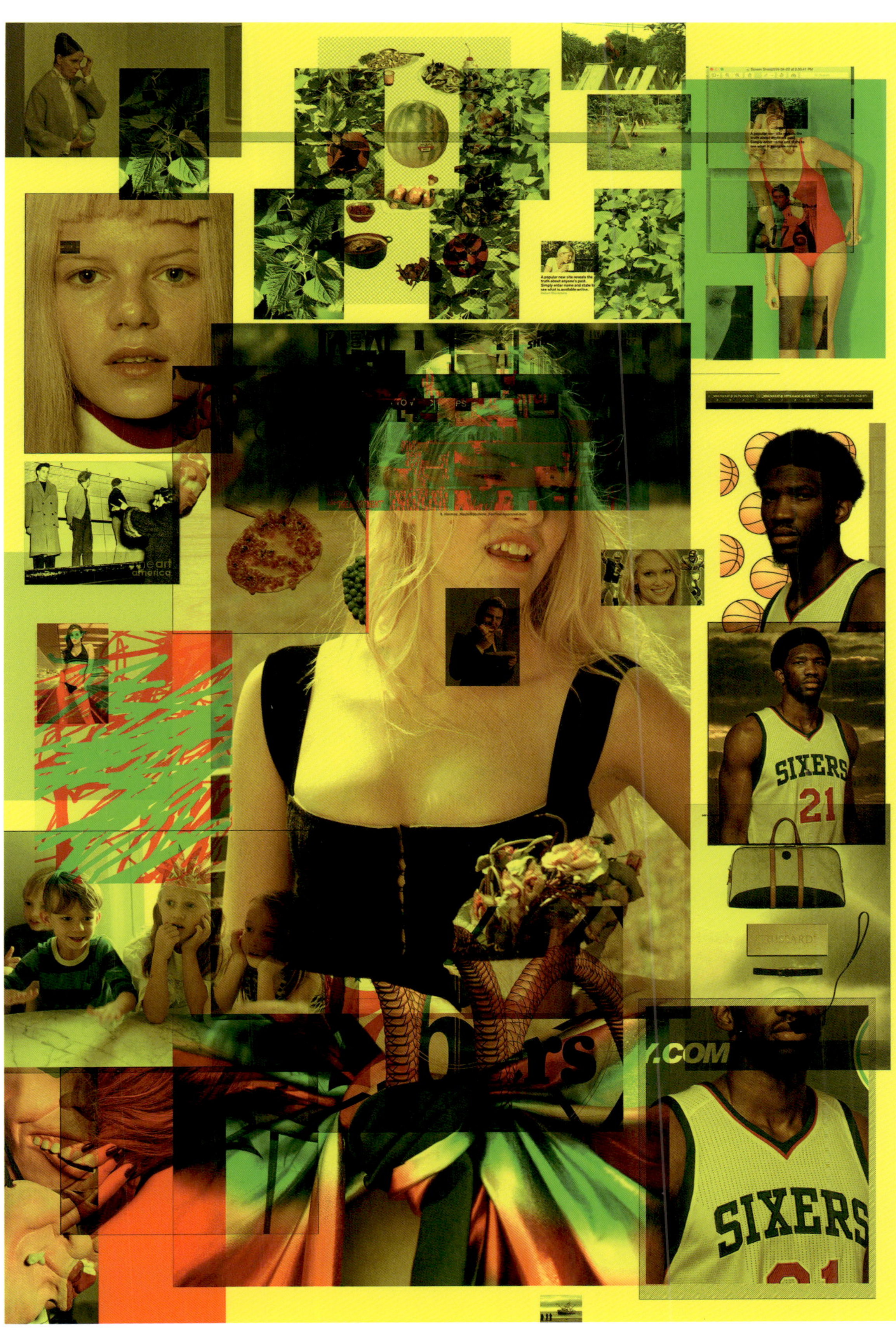
A popular new site reveals the truth about anyone's past. Simply enter name and state to see what is available online.
SIXERS
21
.COM
SIXERS

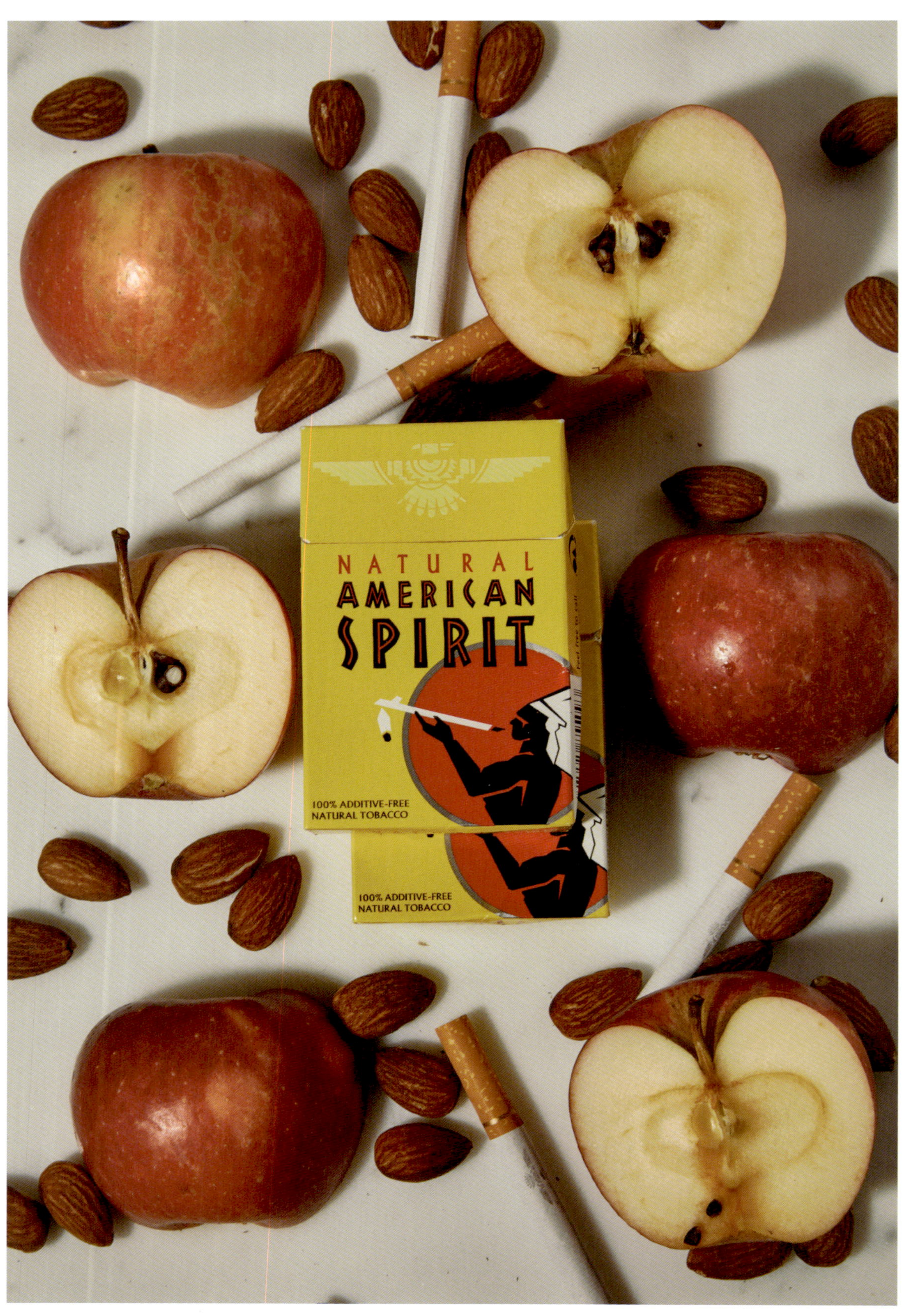
NATURAL
AMERICAN
SPIRIT
100% ADDITIVE-FREE
NATURAL TOBACCO
100% ADDITIVE-FREE
NATURAL TOBACCO

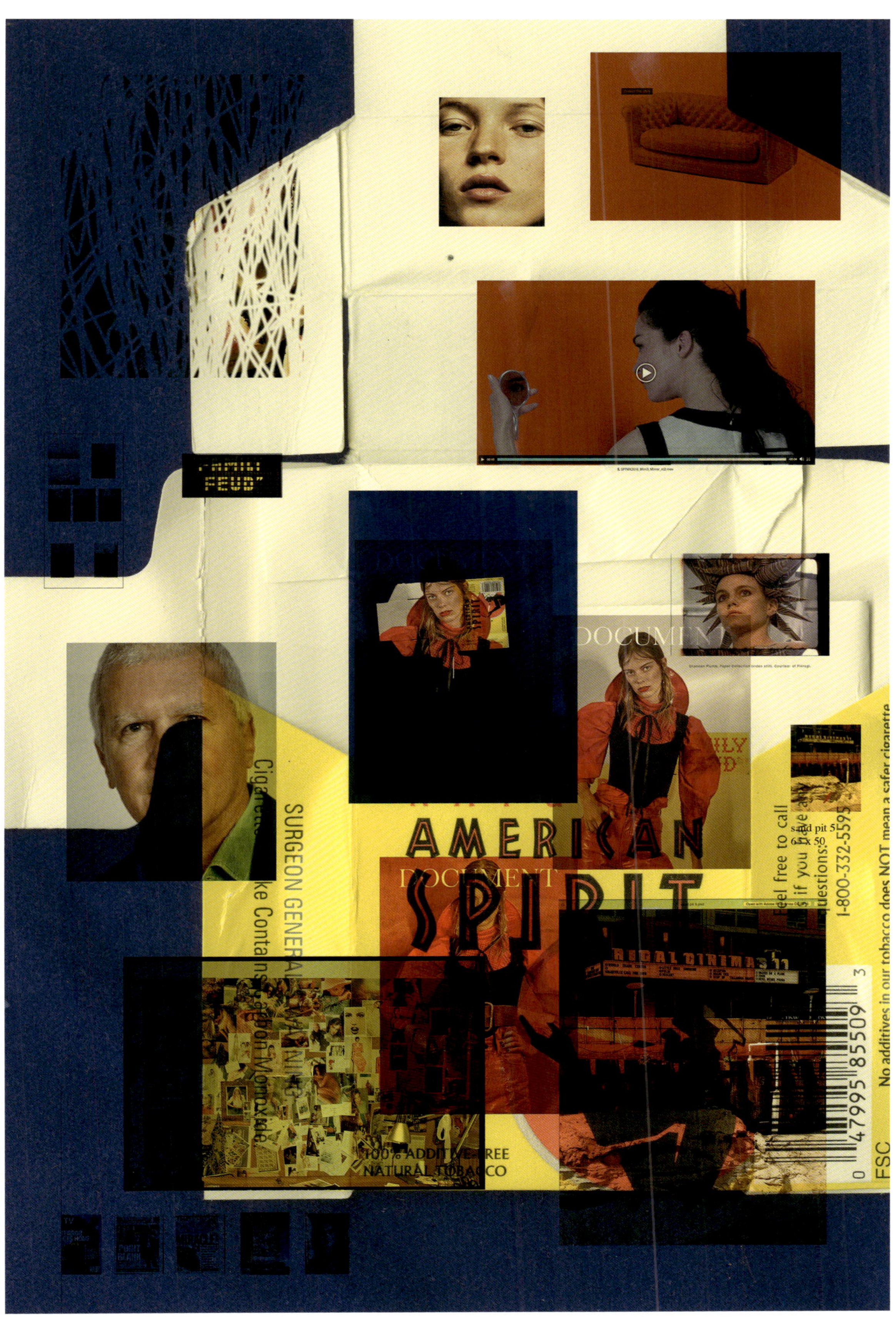
AMERICAN
DOCUMENT
SURGEON GENERAL
100% ADDITIVE-FREE
NATURAL TOBACCO
1-800-332-5595
No additives in our tobacco does NOT mean a safer cigarette
sand pit 5
65 x 50
0 47995 85509 3
FSC

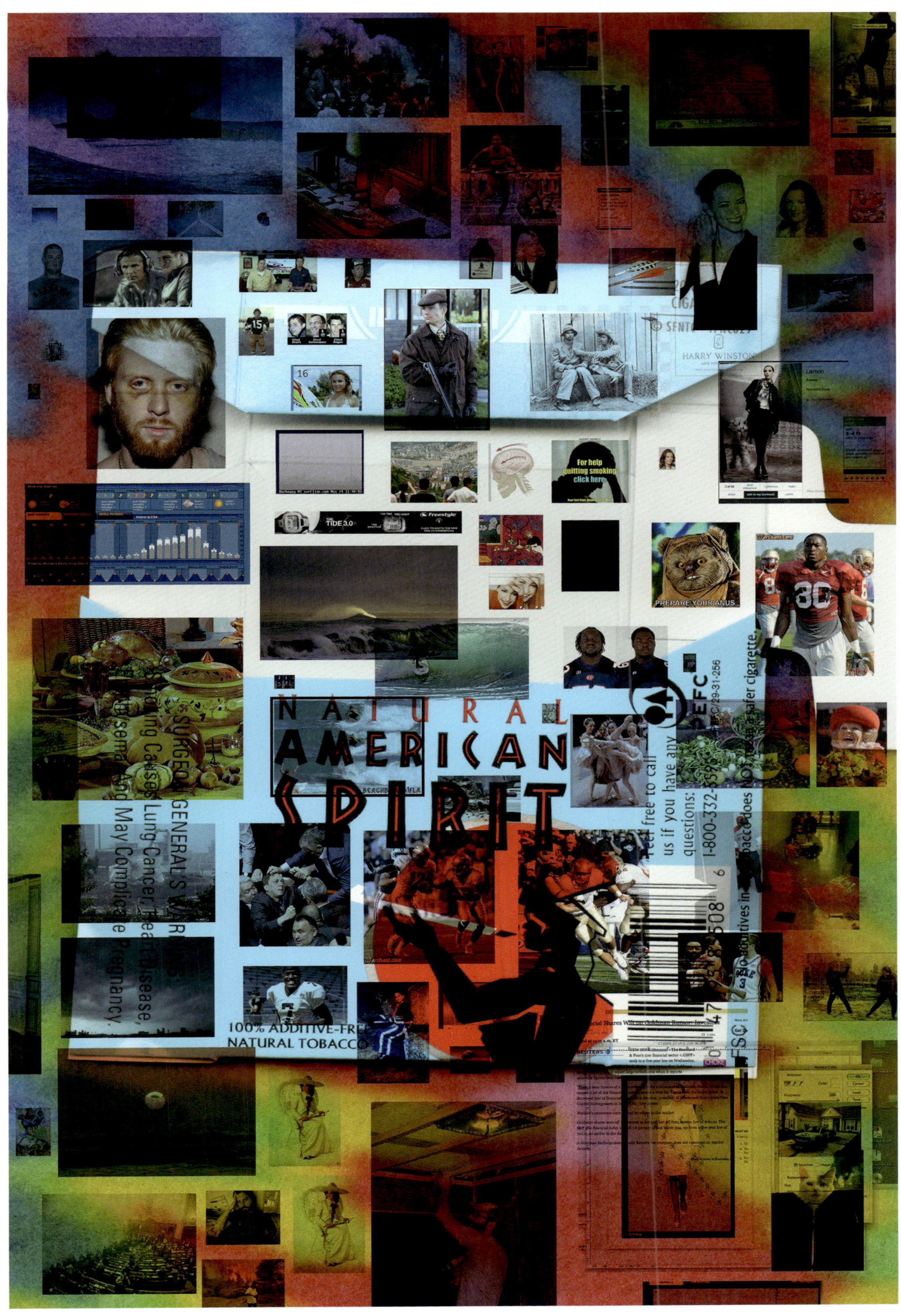

NATURAL
AMERICAN
SPIRIT
100% ADDITIVE-FRE
NATURAL TOBACCO
SURGEON GENERAL'S WARNING:
Smoking Causes Lung Cancer, Heart Disease,
Emphysema, And May Complicate Pregnancy.
Feel free to call
us if you have any
questions:
1-800-332-5595
No additives in our tobacco does NOT mean a safer cigarette.
For help
quitting smoking
click here
PREPARE YOUR ANUS
HARRY WINSTON
TIDE 3.0

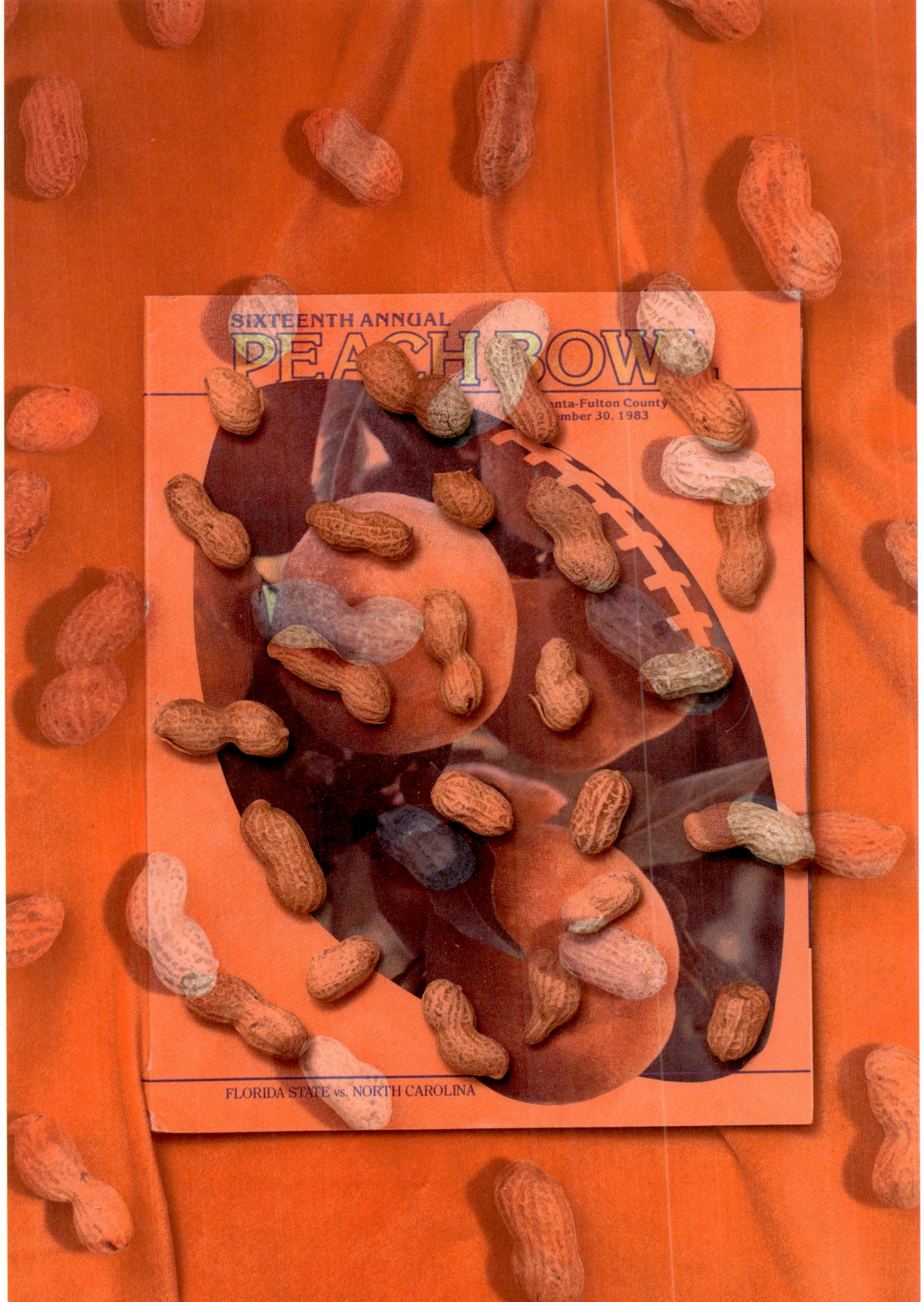
SIXTEENTH ANNUAL
FLORIDA STATE vs. NORTH CAROLINA

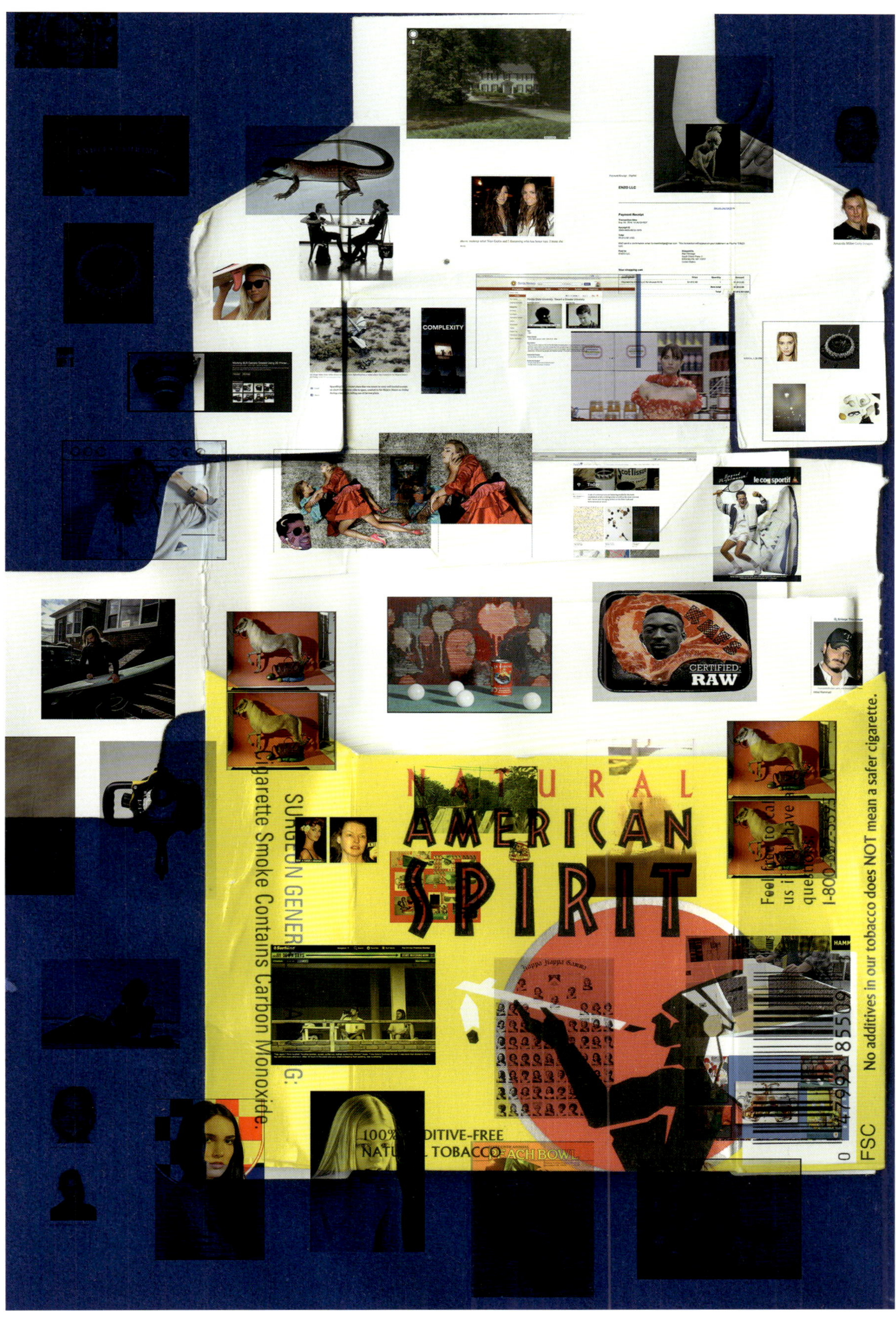

COMPLEXITY
le coq sportif
CERTIFIED RAW
NATURAL
AMERICAN
SPIRIT
SURGEON GENER
Cigarette Smoke Contains Carbon Monoxide.
100%
DITIVE-FREE
NATU
L TOBACCO
No additives in our tobacco does NOT mean a safer cigarette.
FSC

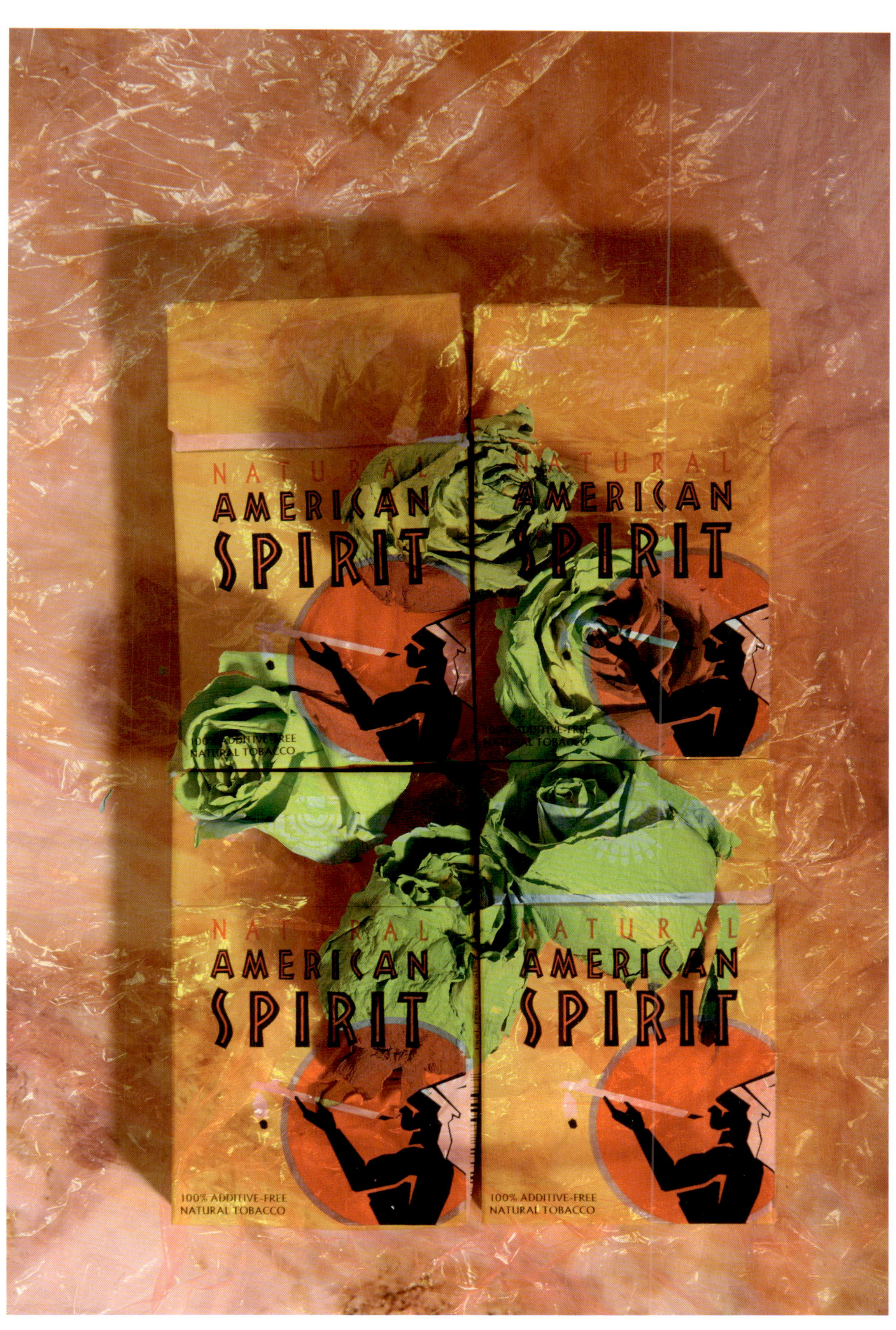
AMERICAN
SPIRIT
NATURAL
AMERICAN
SPIRIT
AMERICAN
SPIRIT
100% ADDITIVE-FREE
NATURAL TOBACCO
NATURAL
AMERICAN
SPIRIT
100% ADDITIVE-FREE
NATURAL TOBACCO

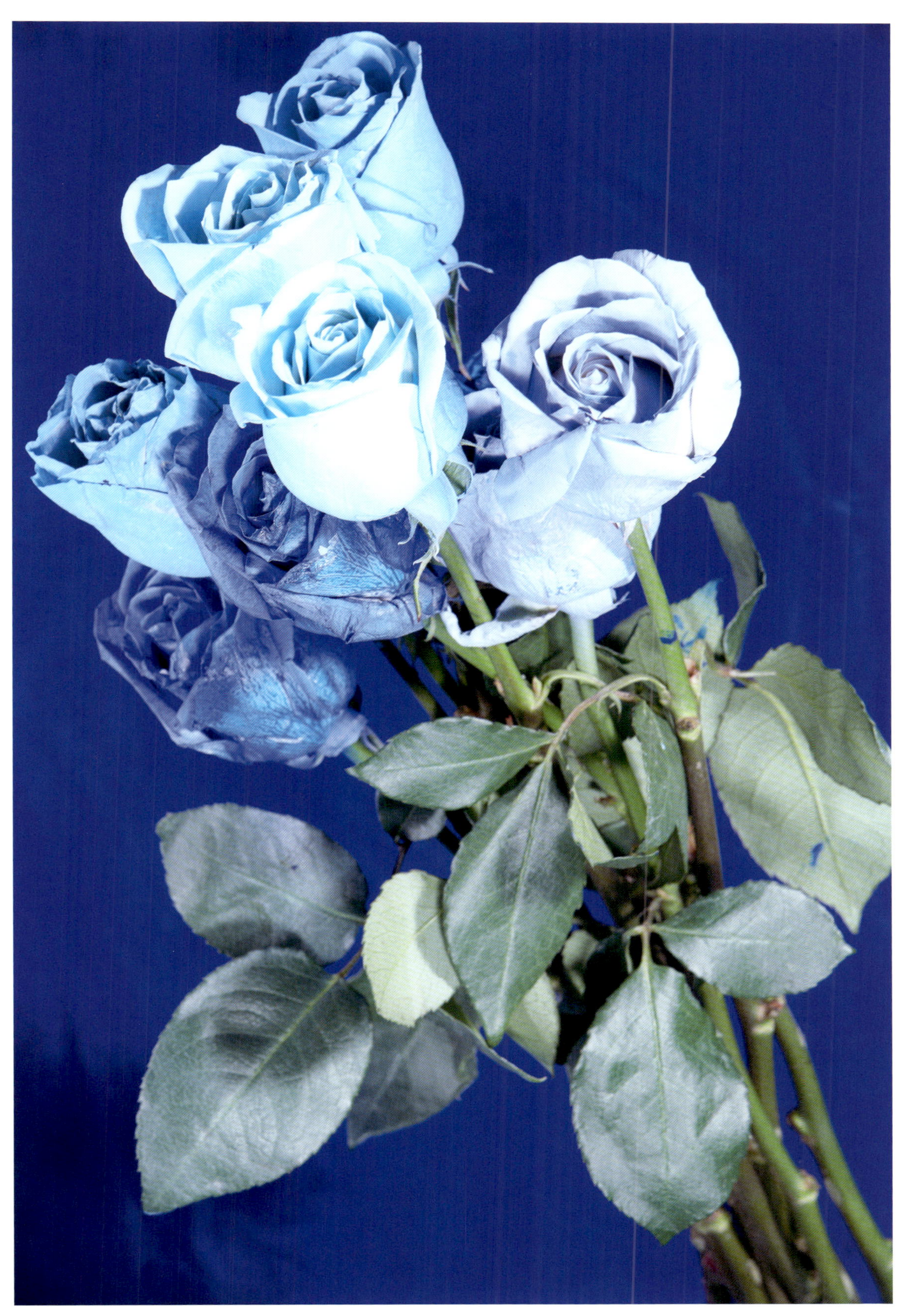

Thank You

Brendan Dugan
David Schoerner
Sinisa Mackovic
Andy Harman
Alicia Burke
Vogue China
Daniella Paudice
Katie Shillingford
Laura Genninger
Another Magazine
Cookie Monster
Lewis Mitchell
David Lane
The Gourmand
Alanna Arrington
Jasper Johns
Mike Ovitz
Abby Champion
Josef Bull
Louise Parker
Andrew WK
Joel Embiid
David Heller
Kadri Vahersalu
Robbie Spencer
Lee Louise
Mariacarla Boscono
Shannon Plumb
Lexi Boling
Larry Gagosian
Auggie
Will Englehardt
Nicole Fasolino
Sigrid and Karmen
Irving Penn
Grace Hartzel
Kenny "Raw" Shaw
David Jimenez
Linda Evangelista
Chubbs
Tabitha Pernar
Dane Reynolds
Craig Robinson
Anne Pontegnie
Ivy Crewdson
Cornelia Grassi
Andrew Kreps
Liz Mulholland
Sam Orlofsky
Barbara Gladstone
Max Falkenstein
Shea Spencer
Felix Frith

Published on the occasion of the exhibition

Roe Ethridge
American Spirit

Andrew Kreps Gallery
537 West 22nd Street
New York, NY 10011
February 23–April 8, 2017

Published by Karma, New York

Second printing of 1,000 copies

ISBN 978-1-942607-67-0